LIVING *through* HISTORY

Britain 1750 – 1900

Nigel Kelly, Rosemary Rees
and Jane Shuter

Acknowledgements

Published in Great Britain by Heinemann Library, Halley Court, Jordan Hill, Oxford OX2 8EJ, a division of Reed Educational and Professional Publishing Ltd.

OXFORD CHICAGO PORTSMOUTH (NH) USA
BLANTYRE MELBOURNE AUCKLAND
IBADAN GABORONE JOHANNESBURG

Heinemann is a registered trademark of
Reed Educational and Professional Publishing Ltd.

© Nigel Kelly, Rosemary Rees and Jane Shuter 1998

The right of Nigel Kelly, Rosemary Rees and Jane Shuter to be identified as the authors of this work has been asserted by them in accordance with Copyright, Designs and Patent Act.

First published 1998

02 01 00 99
10 9 8 7 6 5 4 3 2 1

British Library Cataloguing in Publication Data
Kelly, Nigel, 1954-
    Britain, 1750-1900.- (Living through history)
    1. Great Britain - History - 18th century -
    Juvenile literature 2. Great Britain - History -
    19th century - Juvenile literature
    I. Title II. Rees, Rosemary, 1942- III. Shuter,
    Jane
    941'.07

ISBN 0 431 06855 0 (Hardback)
ISBN 0 431 06854 2 (Paperback)

Designed and produced by Visual Image.
Illustrations by Sally Artz, Stephen Wisdom and Visual Image.

Printed in Spain by Edelvives

Cover photograph: Bridgeman/Manchester City Art Library, Imperial War Museum

Photographic acknowledgements
The authors and publisher would like to thank the following for permission to reproduce photographs:

AKG: 3.5D
Birmingham City Library: p5D
Bradford Libraries: 2.8A, C, 2.9A, B, C, D
Bridgeman: 1.1A, 1.2G, 2.13F, 2.14D, 3.4B, 3.5B,
British Museum: p4A
Cfarthfa Castle: 2.14A, B
Catherine Emmerson: 3.9A
e.t. Archive: 1.1C, 2.1D, 2.2A
Fotomas: 1.6B, 2.5M
Getty Images: 1.4B
Giraudon: 3.3A
Chris Honeywell: 2.5E
Hulton Getty: 1.5B
J. Meakin: 2.3D
Katz: 2.1C, 2.7A
Lancaster City Museums: 1.2D
Mary Evans: p7F, 1.6C, 1.7B, 2.5A, C, D, 2.11A,
2.12F, 2.13A,
Michael Holford: 1.4A
Museum of English Rural Life: 3.9C
National Library of Wales: 3.7B, D
National Portrait Gallery: 1.1B
National Trust: p4B
Paul Revere Memorial Association: 3.2C
PRO: 3.6D
Punch: 2.5H, 3.6C
Quarry Bank Mill: 2.10A, B, C, 2.11B, C
Salvation Army: p6E
Sotheby's: 1.2H
The Science Museum: 2.1A
Thomas Nelson: 1.3A
Topham: 2.1B
Wandsworth Library: p5C
West Sussex Record Office: 2.14C

The publishers have made every effort to trace copyright holders of material in this book. Any omissions will be rectified in subsequent printings if notice is given to the publisher.

CONTENTS

Britain 1750–1900

BRITAIN 1750–1900, AN INTRODUCTION

Events and ideas

If people living in Britain in 1750 had been transported forward in time, they would hardly have recognised Britain in 1900. Many places which had earlier been just villages or small towns were now bustling cities with what seemed to be huge populations. The ways that people got from place to place had also changed. The way **goods** were made and the way land was farmed were very different. During this period Britain began to change from an agricultural country to one which earned its living through selling manufactured goods. This book looks at some of the major events of the period 1750–1900, and gives you an idea of what it was like to live through some of them.

Trade, the force for change?

The driving force behind many of the changes from 1750 onward was trade. Trade made money. Britain expanded its trading ports, fought to defend them, and acquired an empire. It was important to make cheap goods to trade. Machines were invented and constantly improved to make this possible. Factories were built in towns to make production easier. It was important to move trade goods around quickly and cheaply. Roads were improved, canals dug and railways built at an amazing rate. Much of the money put into these developments came from merchants who would benefit from them.

LONDON BEFORE 1850

Source A

Source B

Even the city of London could seem peaceful and rural in the early 1800s. People in St James' Park, in the middle of London, could still buy their milk fresh from the cow. The drawing shows St Martin's Lane in 1825. The church is the church of St Martin's-in-the-Fields.

Industrialisation

One of the most obvious changes that took place was the shift in the way work was done. In 1750 most work was done by small groups of people, using simple equipment. Most people lived in the countryside, and worked on the land. By 1900 a great deal of work was done by machines, many of them in big factories in large towns. Many more people lived in towns, to be close to work. Others were put out of work on the land because of changes in farming.

Industrial towns

When people began to use factories to make things, towns and cities grew. Those that grew fastest were not established places, like London. Instead they were factory towns which sprang up from villages well placed for access to water (for the stages of making cloth) and coal (to power steam engines). One of the fastest growing towns was Bradford. In 1801 about 6000 people lived there. Then factories were set up there. By 1851 there were 104,000 people living there. By 1901 there were 280,000.

LONDON IN ABOUT 1900

By 1900 people bought their milk from dairies (shops that sold milk, cream and butter) or carts that went from door to door. Mr Morrison, owner of the dairy and carts in Source C, had the last herd of cows in London, in 1905. Source D shows Trafalgar Square and the church of St Martin's-in-the-Fields in 1902.

Source C

Source D

Leaving the country

Between 1750 and 1900 about fourteen million people **emigrated**. Many went to live in the USA. Most of the rest went to live in British colonies. Some of these were sent there, **transported** as criminals, rather than leaving of their own free will. But others left because their lives in Britain were so miserable that they wanted to make a new life. Many were encouraged to emigrate by landlords who no longer had work for them. Despite this huge drain of people, there were over five times as many people living in Britain in 1900 as there had been in 1750. Why?

More people, living longer

The population of Britain went up sharply for many reasons. By 1900 many towns had better water supplies and sanitation, this kept people healthier. Medical care was better, and vaccines had been discovered to fight disease. People were generally healthier, so lived longer. Babies were less likely to die as soon as they were born (see Source E).

Source E

Britain 1750 and 1900.

Salvation Army midwives visit a mother at home in 1889. A lot of the help for poor families came from organisations like this.

Colonies

As Britain became more powerful it began to acquire colonies abroad, for example in America and India. These colonies helped produce raw materials for British industries and provided places to sell manufactured goods. Not surprisingly, other countries also wanted colonies, and this led to clashes. Britain and France, for example, were great rivals and frequently went to war over control of colonies.

Unrest at home

This was also a time when many working people began to fight for their rights. Britain watched uneasily as other countries in Europe were rocked by discontent among their working people. In France this errupted into a successful revolution and the execution of the French king. British workers, made uneasy by poor living and working conditions and the growing use of machinery to do their jobs, were also restless. They wanted better working and living conditions, the right to form unions, even the right to vote. The government and factory owners were unwilling to change, but they were shaken by outbreaks of violence around the country. They made just enough changes to calm things down.

French and British ships fighting in the Battle of Trafalgar 1805, during the Napoleonic Wars. As a result of these wars Britain gained new land for its empire.

Things to think about

As you read about the various events in the book ask yourself:

- What do the people involved in the event want?
- What actually happened?
- Was this what they wanted?
- Could they have predicted what would happen?

In 1750 Britain was a major trading nation. Its goods were traded across the world by companies such as the East India Company and the Hudson's Bay Company. But at this time Britain did not actually own large areas of land abroad (with the exception of America, which was to win its independence from Britain in 1783).

By 1900 things had changed. Britain had a huge empire which covered a quarter of the world's land mass. Queen Victoria was recognised as ruler by people as far afield as Canada, Trinidad and Australia. How did this happen?

Reasons for the growth of the Empire

During the eighteenth century most British politicians thought that having an empire was not a good idea. Running colonies abroad would be very expensive, and they would require a large, expensive fleet to protect them. Also, politicians feared that having an empire might lead to war.

But in the second half of the nineteenth century these attitudes began to change as the benefits of controlling land overseas became more apparent.

The trading posts which British merchants controlled in 1750 provided good opportunities to sell British goods abroad and to buy raw materials, such as cotton and tea. If Britain owned more places, it would be easier to export goods there and raw materials could be bought more cheaply.

The spread of beliefs

There were many Britons who believed that their country had a duty to spread its beliefs throughout the world. Britain was the world's most powerful country and the people of Africa, Asia and other areas would benefit from being under British control. Then they could learn about Christianity, and modern developments in science, technology and medicine.

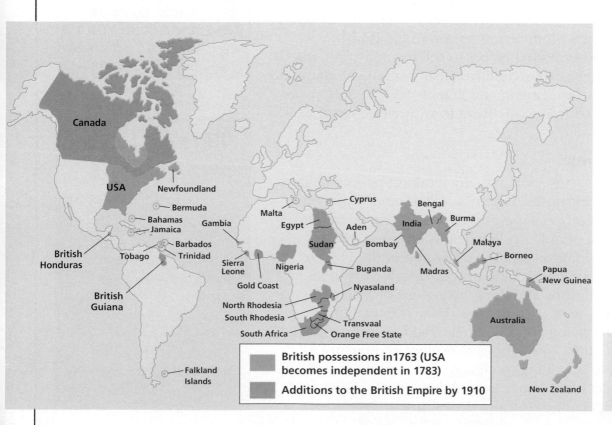

Canada · USA · Newfoundland · Bermuda · Bahamas · Jamaica · Gambia · Malta · Cyprus · Egypt · Aden · Bengal · Burma · India · Bombay · Malaya · Borneo · British Honduras · Tobago · Barbados · Trinidad · Sierra Leone · Nigeria · Sudan · Buganda · Madras · Papua New Guinea · British Guiana · Gold Coast · Nyasaland · North Rhodesia · South Rhodesia · Transvaal · South Africa · Orange Free State · Australia · Falkland Islands · New Zealand

British possessions in 1763 (USA becomes independent in 1783)

Additions to the British Empire by 1910

The British Empire in 1763 and 1910.

Queen Victoria presenting a bible to a foreign prince.

So men such as Cecil Rhodes and David Livingstone went to Africa believing that it was their duty to civilise the local population and teach them the benefits of the British way of life.

The spoils of war

In some ways the British Empire was gained almost by accident. Between 1700 and 1850 Britain won a number of wars which brought colonies as prizes for victory. For instance, Gibraltar was won in the War of Spanish Succession (1701–14). After defeating France and Austria in the Seven Years' War (1756–63), Britain gained Canada and parts of India. When the French Emperor Napoleon was defeated in the Napoleonic Wars in 1815, Britain gained Sri Lanka and parts of South Africa. Hong Kong became a British possession when China was defeated by Britain in the 'Opium Wars' of the nineteenth century.

A stuffed elephant at the Great Exhibition of 1851. This exhibition was set up to show the achievements of Britain in technology and engineering. Over 13,000 exhibits were put on show.

Branching out

Once the British realised the value of an empire, they were quite prepared to fight to keep territories or to gain new ones. So wars of conquest were fought in places such as South Africa, India and Egypt. Other places were gained more easily. Sir Stamford Raffles landed at Singapore in 1819 and negotiated an agreement with the local Sultan to let him build a British base there. In 1770 the explorer James Cook claimed Australia and New Zealand as British possessions and in the 1820s, 3000 convicts a year were being transported to work in Australia.

But Australia was an exception. Other British people who went to live in the Empire were not convicts. They ranged from administrators sent by the government, to merchants realising that the Empire provided an opportunity for making money to those who were attracted by the opportunity to 'start again' in a different land. During the nineteenth century an estimated ten million people emigrated to different parts of the British Empire. Large numbers also went elsewhere in the world, especially to America.

How did having an empire affect trade?

The countries in the Empire were treated as British possessions and there were strict rules about trade. These countries were not allowed to sell their goods to other European countries and had to use British ships to carry their goods. Ports such as London, Liverpool and Bristol built huge docks to handle the trade with the colonies. British trade boomed, sometimes at the expense of trade in the colonies.

Source D

Lieutenant Horace Dorien-Smith explaining in a letter to his local British newspaper how he survived the Battle of Isandhlwana in 1879:

At about ten-thirty the Zulus were seen coming over the hills in thousands. They were in a semi-circle and must have covered several miles of ground. No one knows how many there were, but the general idea was 20,000. Well, to cut a long story short, in half an hour they were right up to camp with bullets flying all over the place. The Zulus nearly all had firearms and lots of ammunition. The place where they seemed thinnest was where we all made for. We had to charge through them and lots of our men were killed there.

Source C

A painting of the Battle of Isandhlwana in 1879. In this battle the Zulus of South Africa defeated the British army. William Gladstone, a leading British politician, complained that the British were fighting the Zulus for committing 'no other offence than their attempt to defend their homes, their wives and families against British artillery with their naked bodies'.

In 1815 India exported thirteen times as much cotton cloth to Britain as it imported. Then Britain put heavy taxes on this cloth. By 1832 British exports of cloth to India were sixteen times what India sold to Britain. The Indian cloth industry had been destroyed to help British cloth merchants.

British merchants also benefited from cheap raw materials from the colonies. Imported sugar, cotton, cocoa and tea were processed in British factories, then resold in Britain or exported to other countries. Goods from the Empire had an impact on the lives of many British people. Wheat came from Canada, and as steamships became more common, food was imported in refrigerated ships. Meat came from South America and dairy products from Australia and New Zealand. New 'exotic' foods, such as bananas and pineapples became common in Britain by 1900.

Another trade made some Britons a lot of money, as you will read in the next unit. Until the slave trade was abolished in the British Empire in 1807 there was a lot of money to be made in the miserable trade in human beings.

Stamford Raffles (1781-1826)

Stamford Raffles was born on a ship off Jamaica. His father was a sea captain trading between Britain and the West Indies.

His father died when Raffles was 14. The boy left school and took a job with the East India Company in London. In his spare time he taught himself languages, such as German and French.

At the age of 24 Raffles became Assistant Governor in Penang in Malaya. Five years later he became Lieutenant-Governor of Java.

It was while he held this office that he gained Singapore for Britain and took the first steps towards building it into a thriving business community. Today a statue stands on the banks of the Singapore river with a plaque commemorating Raffles' 'genius and perception'.

The amount Britain earned from its exports in 1850.

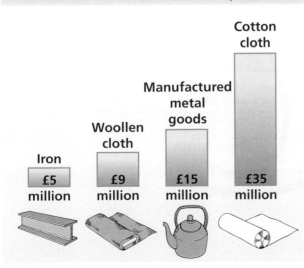

Iron £5 million

Woollen cloth £9 million

Manufactured metal goods £15 million

Cotton cloth £35 million

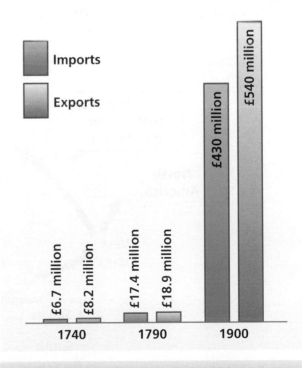

Imports

Exports

	1740		1790		1900	
	£6.7 million	£8.2 million	£17.4 million	£18.9 million	£430 million	£540 million

British imports and exports 1740–1900.

1.2 THE SLAVE TRADE

What was the slave trade?

The slave trade was a trade in people, usually black people, from the west coast of Africa. These people were taken to the West Indies or America and sold to work on **plantations**. **Planters** grew sugar, coffee, tobacco and cotton to meet an ever-growing demand for these things in Britain. The more they could grow, the more money they could make. The British had traded slaves since the 1560s. By 1750 they had a very efficient system.

How did the system work?

Ships left Britain and sailed to West Africa. Here they swapped cloth, guns and alcohol for slaves. The slaves were then taken across the Atlantic to the West Indies. By 1750 there were specially designed ships, made to cram in as many slaves as possible. The conditions aboard these ships were appalling. The slaves were sold, mostly in the West Indies, although some were sold directly in America. Merchants then bought sugar, tobacco, coffee, rum and cotton with the money from selling slaves. They sailed back to Britain and sold these goods in Britain or in other parts of Europe.

Source A

From the Journal of Nicholas Owen, who set up as a slave trader in West Africa in the 1750s:

The people here trade elephant teeth [ivory tusks], slaves and rice for guns, gunpowder and shot, pewter, pans, brass kettles, iron bars and cloth. We purchase slaves for the merchants – a troublesome job. Some merchants dislike this trade, but not many. You have to give people drink and iron bars, then they get slaves for you. You still have to pay for the slaves. You can make enough when trade is quick, but when trade falls off, very few English ships come. Then the slaves pile up and their prices fall.

The slave trade was also known as the triangular trade. The map shows what was traded at each stopping point on the triangle.

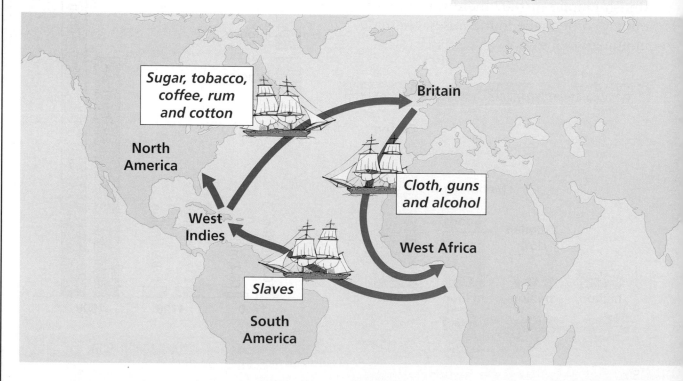

Sugar, tobacco, coffee, rum and cotton

Britain

North America

Cloth, guns and alcohol

West Indies

West Africa

Slaves

South America

Why was the slave trade important?

The slave trade made some merchant families very rich indeed. But it had an effect on the lives of many people who were not directly involved. Slavery made sugar, tobacco and cotton cheaper. More people could afford them. The slave trade helped Britain's trade abroad, because the British could sell their goods, especially cotton cloth, at a good price. Slave traders helped the British economy. They put money from their trade into cotton mills, railways, roads and canals.

Did slavery exist in Britain?

People thought of slavery as something that happened in the colonies. But slaves were bought and sold in Britain too. They were advertised in the papers, next to houses for rent or unwanted furniture. In the eighteenth century some were even made to wear iron collars or chains. Most, however, were treated more like toys than slaves. A little black boy, dressed in silks and a turban, became a rich lady's fashion accessory. Either way, they were not treated as people. They could be sold or simply thrown out, for being sullen or out of fashion, or just for growing up. But as demands for the abolition of the slave trade grew, and as more became known about the conditions slaves suffered, attitudes to slavery changed.

William Wilberforce (1759–1833)

William Wilberforce was born into a family of merchants in Hull, but did not take part in the slave trade. William became MP for Hull. In 1787, aged 28, he was asked to lead the parliamentary protest over slavery. People listened to him, because he was charming and a good speaker. He gained public support, but introduced bill after bill against slavery into parliament, with no success. Ten years later over 50,000 slaves had been bought and sold. In 1807 slavery was abolished.

It's silly to say the slave trade is wrong. They have a better life as slaves, not savages.

Besides, we don't encourage it, do we? Pour more tea James!

1750

Have you read Equiano's story of being a slave? And heard Mr Granville Sharp?

It's just one slave's bad experience. As for Granville Sharp, I'm told he's been misled.

1790

Where's James?

I gave him his freedom. Granville Sharp has shown he was right. I've read these pamphlets that show slavery is wrong. Pour more tea Betty!

1791

Are you going to the abolitionist meeting this afternoon?

Of course! Everyone with any sense knows slavery is wrong – have you seen the latest newspaper article?

1795

Changing attitudes to slavery.

Trading in misery

So who traded in slaves? There were several sorts of slave traders. The ones who made the most money from the trade were families who had plantations in the West Indies and owned slaves themselves. They often had several family members involved in the trade, and socialised and married into other families in the same business. In this way they lived in their own little bubble, cut off from the rising number of people in Britain who were **abolitionists** (wanted slavery abolished). But they did not ignore the criticism.

Justifying slavery

Rich slave traders wrote a great deal, in books and letters to the papers, telling people how the well-meaning interference of abolitionists sprang from a complete misunderstanding of the situation. They had never been to plantations, did not understand slavery (which was really *good* for black people) and did not understand black people. They also pointed out how bad abolition would be for British trade.

Source C

Ordinary people with savings that they wanted to increase also took part in the slave trade. In 1795 a Liverpool man wrote:

Almost every man in Liverpool is a merchant. Many of the small ships that carry but a hundred slaves are kitted out by lawyers, drapers, rope-makers, grocers, barbers and tailors, all hoping to make a profit on the voyage.

Source D

In 1788 the poet William Cowper summed up why people tried to ignore the evils of slavery.

**I admit I am shocked at the purchase of slaves,
And fear those who buy them and sell them are knaves;
What I hear of their hardships, their tortures, and groans,
Is almost enough to draw pity from stones!
I pity them greatly, but I must be mumm [quiet],
For how could we do without sugar and rum?**

Source B

Trading ports

Some ports grew into thriving cities on the profits of the slave trade. Liverpool and Hull, Bristol and Lancaster all grew quickly once the triangular trade was set up. As well as trade in sugar and crops from America and the West Indies, the ports also got a lot of work building and repairing boats for the trade.

Dodshon Foster was a merchant in Lancaster who was involved in the slave trade. Trading in slaves was a quick way to riches and to respectability. Several men who became rich from the slave trade in Lancaster also became mayors of the city.

THE LONG FAMILY

Samuel Long set up a sugar plantation in Jamaica when he arrived, aged 17, with the English army in 1655. When he died, in 1683, he left two plantations and possessions worth £12,000 – a great deal of money at the time.

Samuel's son, Charles, moved to England in 1700. This was a bad move. A friend wrote to Charles (in 1707) that his house in Jamaica needed repair, his crops were neglected, his slaves hardly fed – everything was falling apart. He said Charles should come back. He never did. He was making enough money anyway.

By this time other members of the family were running Jamaican plantations. One of these was Samuel Long II (nephew of the first Samuel Long). He had lands in Jamaica, Cornwall and London. His son Edward took over when he died in 1757. Edward was brought up in Britain. But he fitted in quickly in Jamaica. Family connections and his training in the law meant he became a judge in the courts, as well as a plantation owner. He married the only daughter of Thomas Beckford, the richest slave owner in Jamaica (grandson of a man who came to Jamaica in 1655, like Samuel Long). Edward Long is famous for his writings which defend plantation owning and slavery.

Long retired to England in 1769, because of ill-health. He had foolish ideas about the inferiority of black people. He wrote:

*I think there are extremely good reasons for believing that the White and the Negro are two distinct species. Black people do not have hair, but a covering of wool. They have a bestial [animal like] smell. They have no plan or system of **morality**. They are cruel to their children. When we look at their dissimilarity to the rest of mankind, must we not conclude that they are different? Indeed they have more in common with the orangutan.*

Source E

Milling sugar in Antigua. This illustration comes from a book about travels in the West Indies. It may be accurate about the process of milling sugar in the early 1800s, but the slaves are too well dressed, too unhurried, too clean and too well fed for the picture to be an accurate reflection of life on a sugar plantation.

Lancaster

Lancaster was not as large a port as Hull or Liverpool. Yet all three ports follow the same pattern of growth and dependence on the slave trade.
Ships owned by Lancaster merchants:
1709: 1,000 tonnes
1751: 2,300 tonnes
1791: 10,700 tonnes
In 1720 about five ships a year were involved in the slave trade. By 1780 it was 30.

Black people in Britain

Slaves were mostly confined to overseas plantations. This did not mean that there were no black people in Britain. They came back with plantation owners who wanted to settle in Britain. They also came as sailors or as servants. Many arrived as slaves. Here are the experiences of just a few of them.

FRANCIS BARBER

Not all black servant-children were turned out of the house when they grew up (see page 13). Some became part of the family. Francis Barber was born a slave in Jamaica. In 1750, when he was still a boy, he came to Britain as Captain Bathurst's servant. Bathurst had Barber educated. When he died, in 1752, he gave Barber his freedom. Barber went to work for Dr Johnson, a friend of Bathurst. Johnson let Barber carry on with his education. He let him get married in 1776. When Johnson died, in 1782, he left Barber all his property. Barber and his wife set up a school in Staffordshire which they ran until Barber died in 1801. His wife then ran the school alone.

Runaways

People put adverts in newspapers asking for help in tracking down runaway slaves:

Hannah Press, a serving maid of middle height and brown complexion, wearing a light gown and petticoat and a dark riding hood, speaking broad Yorkshire, ran away from service Sunday, 2 March. She took with her a silver tankard, a silver plate, six silver forks, six silver spoons.

John Bowman, apprentice to John Ibbett, ran away from his master Monday last. He is about 19 years of age, brown complexion about 5' 3" high. He has a sullen look and wears a dark brown wig and a blue coat.

Run away from his master, a Negro boy, under five feet high, about 16 years old. Named Charles. He is bow-legged, hollow-backed and pot-bellied.

Steps to freedom in Britain

1772 Slaves cannot be taken out of Britain against their will.
1807 Slave trade abolished.
1833 Slavery abolished in British colonies.

Source F

In the 1750s it was very fashionable to have black children as servants, as this painting shows.

JAMES SOMERSET

James Somerset came to Britain in 1769. He was brought as a slave by his American master, Charles Stewart. In 1771 he ran away. He hid in London's free black community. Stewart tracked Somerset down. He had him kidnapped and given to the captain of the ship *Ann and Mary*, which was due to sail for Jamaica. He told the captain to lock Somerset up, take him to Jamaica and sell him.

Granville Sharp, who was one of the earliest British abolitionists, heard about the case. He wanted to bring the case to law. He said he needed Somerset as a witness, so he could not be taken from the country. The case was taken to court, under the argument that, while the colonies accepted slavery, it was not part of British law. So, the defence lawyer said, once slaves set foot on English soil they were under British law, and free. The judge, Lord Mansfield, tried hard to make people settle the case out of court. He was under a lot of pressure: *I am told there are no less than 15,000 slaves now in England, who will desire their liberty if the law decides in favour of this case. This will cost their owners some £700,000. Yet if we allow ourselves to be ruled by the laws of the colonies, the implications are yet worse.* On 22 June 1772, Mansfield gave his decision: *Slavery was never in use in this country. It is so odious that it cannot be supported on moral, or political grounds. Whatever inconvenience may follow from this decision, the black man is freed.* We know that Somerset was freed, but not what happened to him after.

SOMERSET CASE: JUDGE FREES THE BLACK MAN

It's a good thing. Maybe they'll treat us like people now.

They'll just be more scared and want to get rid of us.

My master was angry. He beat me.

They'll be nothing but trouble, now. What if they riot?

We'll all be murdered in our beds! Get them out of the country.

I'll lose a fortune if I have to free mine!

Fears and rumours.

Steps to abolition in Britain

In 1807 the slave trade was abolished in Britain. This does not mean that slavery was abolished, just that it was illegal for British merchants to trade in slaves. It did not free British slaves. Nor did it free the large numbers of slaves in British colonies, like the West Indies, that depended on slave labour. Slavery was abolished in British lands in 1833. Even then, slaves could not leave at once but had to work as 'apprentices' for their masters for seven more years.

17

During the eighteenth century the British began to take an interest in trade with India. Indian goods such as textiles, **indigo** and spices could be sold at a good profit in Britain. A group of merchants formed the East India Company, which was given sole rights to trade in India by the British government. In return, the East India Company agreed to give the British government a share of its profits.

The French also formed an East India Company and the two rival companies were forced to have their own small army to protect their trade in India. Then in 1756 Britain and France went to war. The French encouraged the ruler of Bengal, Nawab Saraj ud-Daulah, to attack the British base at Calcutta. What happened next has become part of British history, but no one is really sure how true it is.

The Hole

The story goes that in 1756 Saraj ud-Daulah attacked and captured the English settlement at Calcutta. He imprisoned 146 English prisoners in a notorious military prison which was only about 8 metres by 6 metres. The room was so small and so short of air that by the next morning 123 of the prisoners had died. The story of the 'Black Hole of Calutta' appeared in British children's history books for much of the eighteenth and nineteenth centuries.

There are, however, one or two problems with the story. It comes from the writings of a survivor, John Holwell, who was a British official in the area. Holwell describes how, as soon as the prisoners were thrust into the small room, they began to sweat profusely and soon developed a raging thirst. It was not long before everyone was 'giving way to the violence of their passions' and fighting each other, even killing people, in an effort to get to the one small window. Indian historians have since carried out investigations into the episode. They believe that the numbers killed in the prison were much lower, or even that the event never took place at all.

Some interesting facts about the Black Hole of Calcutta

- The prison was already called the 'Black Hole' before the events of 1756.
- An Indian history book written a few years after the event lists attacks on the English by Indians, but does not mention the Black Hole of Calcutta.
- No report of the event was ever made to the Directors of the East India Company.
- In 1757 leaders from Britain and India signed the Treaty of Alingar in which the Indians agreed to pay compensation for attacks on British citizens. No mention was made of the Black Hole of Calcutta.

A cartoon version of the Black Hole published in a recent British school history book.

> **12** MEANWHILE, IN INDIA: Another Indian prince, Suraj-ud-Dowlah, tried to drive out the East India Company. On 20 June 1756, he captured Calcutta in the north of India, and threw 146 Britons into prison.

> **13** **Source A**
>
> WATER, FOR GOD'S SAKE!

THE BLACK HOLE OF CALCUTTA
Shut all night in a tiny room, without water, all but 23 of the 146 Britons died.

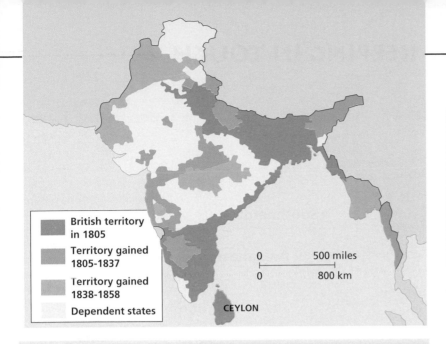

■	British territory in 1805
■	Territory gained 1805-1837
■	Territory gained 1838-1858
	Dependent states

0   500 miles
0   800 km

CEYLON

The establishment of British control in India 1757–1900.

Defeat for the Nawab

Whether or not there is any truth in the story of the Black Hole of Calcutta, Nawab Saraj ud-Dauluh did not profit from his attack on Calcutta. On 23 June 1757, Robert Clive led a force of the East India Company against the Nawab at a small village called Plassey. The so-called 'battle' lasted only a few hours and its outcome was decided before the armies met. Most of the Nawab's army had been bribed to change sides and he was easily defeated. Saraj ud-Dauluh's body was found in a nearby river a few days later.

India becomes a British colony

Following the victory at Plassey, the British steadily gained more control of India and by 1763 the French had been driven from the country. During the next century Britain took control of much of India. After a mutiny by Indian soldiers in the British army in 1857, the British government decided to take direct control of the country instead of allowing the East India Company to run affairs. In 1877 Queen Victoria was given the title Empress of India and a **viceroy** was put in charge of the government of India. India's wealth was so important to Britain that India has often been referred to as 'the jewel in the crown' of the British Empire.

India remained a British possession until it was given its independence in 1947. This independence, however, came only after a long campaign by people such as Mahatma Gandhi, and after determined efforts by the British to stop protests against their rule, such as at Amritsar.

ROBERT CLIVE

Robert Clive's victory at Plassey has earned him the title 'The Father of India'. Following his victory he returned to England in 1760 and, using money he received from gifts and bribes in India, he bought himself a seat as an MP. He was made a baron in 1764 and returned to India to become Governor of Bengal. Ill-health led him to return to England in 1773, where his opponents arranged an investigation into his behaviour in India, accusing him of '**plundering** Bengal'. He was **acquitted**, but the disgrace, coupled with an addiction to opium, led him to take his own life in 1775.

Queen Victoria (1819–1901)

Victoria was the granddaughter of George III and became Queen when her uncle, William IV, died without having any children. By the time of her death she had reigned for 64 years and was one of the best known figures in the world.

During her reign Britain became the most powerful country in the world and Victoria ruled over a quarter of the world's population. In 1877 she was made 'Empress of India', a title of which she was very proud.

How did Britain keep in touch with its growing empire? For much of the period we are studying there was only one answer – letters. From 1850 one of the fastest ways to carry things around the world was on the new steamships. One of the companies set up to take letters, and passengers, all over the Empire was the Peninsular and Oriental Steam Navigation Company – P & O for short. The P & O competed with other companies to carry government mail, soldiers and almost anything else!

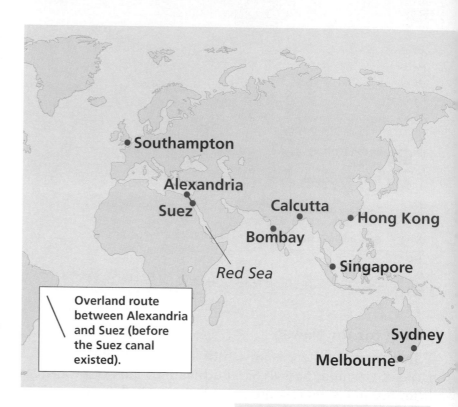

Southampton

Alexandria

Suez

Calcutta

Bombay

Hong Kong

Red Sea

Singapore

Sydney

Melbourne

Overland route between Alexandria and Suez (before the Suez canal existed).

Frank Kendall

Frank Kendall joined P & O in 1856, aged 17. He worked in the Southampton office for two years. In 1858 he was sent to Bombay and then Calcutta, Singapore, Hong Kong and Melbourne. Kendall married in 1867 and had six sons and a daughter. He returned to London in 1881. Kendall retired in 1906 and died a year later. All but one of his sons spent most of their lives working abroad. One of them, Herbert, worked for P & O. Here are extracts from just a few of Frank Kendall's letters home, written in 1858 and 1859.

The places where Frank Kendall worked for P & O.

The *Great Eastern* steam ship, which laid the first telegraph cable under the Atlantic.

Insights

Frank Kendall's letters give us glimpses of more things than just the places Frank went. We learn that P & O shipped live animals as food for their passengers. We find out that Frank's work needed a strong stomach, calm nerves and the willingness to be moved around whenever the company wanted you somewhere else!

Source A

Extract 1
1858: From Southampton to Bombay

17 February: We made it to Gibraltar in just under five days. The soldiers have plenty of room. Many ships this size would cram in 700 or 800 soldiers, but we only have 250. The boat has been **pitching.** The ducks do not like it and quack loudly. They are seasick and get thinner each meal. Sheep are much better passengers.

28 February: We arrived at Alexandria and went to Suez with the troops by train. At the end of the railway we went the 25 miles to Suez by donkey.

9 March: We arrived at Aden to hear the Ava was lost, along with the Calcutta mail. The ship was worth £70,000. P & O will have to pay for the lost cargo. She was also bringing a new shaft for the Alma, which will have to wait for another one and spend even longer laid up. But the Company loses only about three ships a year and hardly any lives are lost at all.

18 March: We arrived in Bombay the night before last. I went to the office yesterday and was put to work at once. Very busy.

Extract 2
1858: Working in Bombay

20 March: There are three others in the office with me and about a dozen native workers. I went to the docks and met the Electric Telegraph people, who say it should not be hard to lay cable through the Red Sea, then we will be able to speak to England in a matter of hours!

23 March: I share a house with 3 others. My servant can speak no English. I speak little Hindustani. But he is said to be good. Servants here do not cheat their masters, but the natives will, in general, never tell the truth if they can lie.

19 June: The drainage in Bombay is awful. When the monsoon rains come, the streets are one big sewer. There are people who are supposed to make sure the streets are cleared, but they don't do it. Cholera, dysentery and fever are all rife. Everything gets damp and mouldy in this weather; except for the metal – which goes rusty!

Extract 3
1859: Suez and Australia

In 1859 Frank was sent, as a **Purser,** from Bombay to Australia via Suez, to learn more about how P & O ships were run.

28 March: At Suez. The passengers transferring to our ship came, with much grumbling about delays, gales and missing luggage. At last we got everything stowed and sailed. One morning there was a cry of 'Man overboard!' The ship stopped. The poor fellow was just visible, some three miles off. By the time the lifeboat got there he was gone. Sharks, probably.

21 April: At Aden. The Emeu had a broken shaft. The Granada will take the mail and passengers – they will reach England a week or more late. We left with 240 tons of coal, in every corner and all over the deck, for the long leg of our journey.

14 May: Sydney harbour is beautiful. Sydney and Melbourne have fine buildings, very fine shops and markets where things are much cheaper than in Bombay. They have a real 'go ahead' feel. Australia is a wonderful country. I would go there tomorrow, if P & O asked me. But I do not wish to become a Purser; it is not the life for me.

12 July: I see the Telegraph is now laid to Aden. So you will hear of our return to Bombay before you get this letter.

Kendall returned to Bombay on 10 September. He was sent to Singapore (the Telegraph followed him!) then Hong Kong in 1863 and Bombay in 1864. He eventually got his wish to live in Australia. He was sent to Melbourne in 1865, where he stayed until he retired.

In the sixteenth century the English government began transporting persistent beggars to the colonies overseas. In the reign of Charles II this practice was extended to include criminals of all kinds. A sentence of transportation to the American colonies meant that such people were 'out of harm's way'.

But in 1783 the American colonies won their independence from Britain and so a new dumping ground for criminals had to be found. An ideal place soon emerged. In 1770 James Cook had landed on the Australian coastline at Botany Bay, claimed it for Britain and renamed it 'New South Wales'.

Source A

Punishments received for various crimes at Gloucester Assizes in 1826.

William James: for breaking into a house and stealing 20 pounds of cheese: 7 years' transportation.

Thomas James: for house-breaking and stealing shirts etc.: Death.

George Cooke: for house-breaking and stealing a quilt: 7 years' transportation.

James Turner: For robbing J. Underwood of a hat on the highway: Death.

Sarah Mears: for receiving 24 bottles of wine knowing them to be stolen: 14 years' transportation.

William Chivers: for breaking into a house and stealing 21 cheeses: 7 years' transportation.

Richard Mee: for stealing a bottle of brandy: 7 years' transportation.

George Goode: for killing T. Hawkins: 18 months' imprisonment.

Elizabeth Jones: for stealing calico and other crimes: Transportation for life.

Richard Fowler: for stealing hay: 12 months' imprisonment.

Cook reported that the new continent was suitable for 'hardy pioneers' to settle and the British Prime Minister, William Pitt, decided to set up a colony of convicts at Botany Bay.

First arrivals

The first fleet of ships, carrying 759 convicts (568 men and 191 women) together with 200 **marines** to guard them, arrived at Botany Bay in January 1788. Captain Arthur Phillip described Botany Bay as 'a poor and sandy heath full of swamps' and so landed further up the coast. Here on 26 January (now known as Australia Day) he began to build a settlement, which he named 'Sydney' after the Home Secretary, Lord Sydney.

It seems strange to think that what is today a mighty nation was for many years known in Britain merely as a **penal colony** for unwanted convicts. Between 1788 and 1868, when transportation ended, about 150,000 convicts were transported to New South Wales, Western Australia and Van Diemen's Land (modern-day Tasmania).

Not all dangerous criminals

The convicts transported to Australia were not all serious criminals. Some were convicted of nothing more than petty crimes, such as stealing cheese or handkerchiefs. Others were well-educated and wealthy people who had committed crimes such as forgery. Some 20% of those transported were women, many of them prostitutes. There was also a large number of Irish people, banished from their homeland after an uprising against the British in 1798. There were also 'political prisoners' whose beliefs had landed them in trouble. Perhaps the best known of these were the Tolpuddle Martyrs, whom you will read about on pages 24–5.

Source B

A nineteenth-century drawing showing convicts being transported to Australia.

James Cook (1728–1779)

Cook, one of England's most famous explorers, was a farm labourer's son from Cleveland who joined the Royal Navy and showed great skill in navigation and map making.

In 1768 he set out, in command of the *Endeavour*, to survey newly discovered Tahiti. From there he sailed on to New Zealand and Australia before returning to England in 1771.

He led two more expeditions, one to the South Pacific in 1772 and one to North America in 1777. On this last expedition he was killed by natives in Hawaii.

But many of those transported to Australia were very poor, with little education and few skills. This explains the appalling treatment they received during the crossing and on arrival. In 1790 the *Neptune* set sail with 502 convicts, of whom 158 died before they reached Australia. The government was forced to pay a bonus on future voyages for each convict safely landed to make sure treatment improved. Even so, treatment was harsh; prisoners were always shackled and **floggings** were common. In Australia conditions could be almost as bad. Flogging was a common penalty with up to 200 lashes being given for theft. Individual convicts were assigned to private employers who often treated them as slaves. However, for some enterprising convicts with a sympathetic master there was the opportunity to 'start again' and make a success of their lives.

Source C

The story of James Pollock, transported to Van Diemen's Land and sent to work for a cruel master.

I did not know what to do; I walked away from the house. My master took up a loaded gun and followed me and swore that he would shoot me if I did not come back. I still went on, for at the time I did not care whether he shot me or not.

The next day I was reported as missing and after four days in the bush with nothing to eat I was captured by a constable. When I appeared before the magistrate my master said how well he treated me and what an idle fellow I was. So the magistrate sentenced me to fifty lashes.

I was then sent back and my master put me to work carrying logs on my back. He was more cruel than ever and I was determined not to stay with him. I ran away four times and got fifty lashes each time.

Finally I was sentenced to fifty lashes more, three months working on the chain gang and then to go back to my master. When I was tied to the triangle to be lashed, my back was in such a mess that the doctor told them to flog me across my breeches.

The Tolpuddle Martyrs

On a cold, grey February morning in 1834, in the tiny Dorset village of Tolpuddle, George Loveless strode out vigorously to his work down the village street, quite unaware of the cruel fate that awaited him. It came in the shape of the parish constable, who on that fateful morning was required to undertake the distasteful duty of arresting his friend and neighbour, George.

The constable stopped him. 'I have a warrant from the magistrates for your arrest, Mr Loveless.'

'For me?'

'Yes, and for others beside you: James Hammett, Thomas Standfield and his son John, young Brine and for your brother, James.'

'What is the warrant for?' asked Loveless. 'What have we done?'

'You'd best take it and read for yourself' was the reply.

Loveless read the warrant, which charged him and his companions with having participated in the taking of an illegal oath. At the request of the constable, Loveless accompanied him to the cottages of the other men. Then the six of them, in the custody of the constable, marched towards the dreadful ordeal which awaited them at the end of the seven miles' walk to Dorchester.

Source D

The notice issued by Dorchester magistrates two days before the arrest of the Tolpuddle Martyrs.

This account of the arrest of six Dorsetshire farm labourers comes from a book published by the Trades Union Congress (TUC) in 1934. To the TUC the labourers were heroes and the book itself is called 'The book of the **Martyrs** of Tolpuddle'. But it is not just the TUC that thinks so highly of the men. Historians also call them 'The Tolpuddle Martyrs'. Who were they, and why are they considered martyrs?

In the early nineteenth century, conditions for many agricultural labourers were appalling. (You can read more about this in the section on the 'Captain Swing' riots, on page 89). It was not uncommon for families of eleven persons to live in a one-roomed cottage just three metres square. Wages were about ten shillings (50p) a week and the standard of living was so low that farm labourers were said to live on 'tea and potatoes'.

Wages in the Tolpuddle area were nine shillings (45p) a week and the local labourers, led by George Loveless, asked for a rise to ten shillings. The farm owners refused and to teach the labourers a lesson they reduced wages first to eight shillings (40p) and then to seven shillings (35p). The men decided to form a trade union to protect themselves. In October 1833 they set up 'The Friendly Society of Agricultural Labourers'. New members of the union had to go through a joining ceremony and swear an oath of allegiance to the union.

It was not illegal to join a trade union, but the authorities disliked working people joining together. It was only a few years since there had been a revolution in France and mutinies in the British navy. So when local magistrates heard about the Tolpuddle union they wrote to the Home Secretary, Lord Melbourne, to ask for advice. He told them to use the law banning people from taking 'illegal oaths' – passed in 1797 to stamp out the navy mutiny.

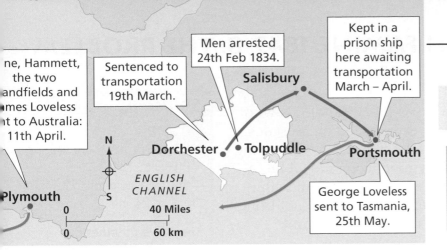

On the map:

ne, Hammett, the two ...andfields and ...mes Loveless ...t to Australia: 11th April.

Sentenced to transportation 19th March.

Men arrested 24th Feb 1834.

Kept in a prison ship here awaiting transportation March – April.

Salisbury

Dorchester • **Tolpuddle**

Portsmouth

N / S

ENGLISH CHANNEL

Plymouth

0 — 40 Miles
0 — 60 km

George Loveless sent to Tasmania, 25th May.

The arrest and transportation of the Tolpuddle Martyrs.

The local magistrates announced that taking an oath to join a union was illegal. Two days later they arrested Loveless and his five colleagues. The men had not known they were breaking the law when they took their oath, but they were found guilty and on 19 March were sentenced to seven years' transportation.

To Australia

On 27 March five of the labourers (George Loveless was too ill to travel) were taken in chains to a prison ship in Portsmouth Harbour. They were transferred to a convict ship and on 11 April set sail for Australia. On 17 August, after a voyage of 111 days, they arrived at Sydney Harbour. They remained on board for three weeks before going to convict barracks in the town. From there they were sent to carry out their seven years of hard labour.

George Loveless was better by 5 April, but he did not join the others. He was taken in chains to Portsmouth and on 25th May set sail for Van Diemen's Land (Tasmania), 700 miles from where his colleagues had been sent.

Pardon and return

The sentence passed on the Tolpuddle Martyrs was very unpopular in Britain and there were many protest meetings. Lawyers and some MPs criticised the judge and said that the conviction was not legal. On 21 April 1834 more than 50,000 people marched in protest in London. In June the new Home Secretary, Lord John Russell, offered to give pardons to four of the men after two years (but not George and James Loveless, who were considered ringleaders). Eventually, in March 1836, the government gave a free pardon to all six men. Even then it was almost a year before they came home and two years before James Hammett was found and returned to Tolpuddle. He remained in Tolpuddle for the rest of his life. The other five emigrated to Canada in 1844 to start a new life.

Source E

From a speech made by George Loveless at the trial:

My Lord, if we have violated any law, it was not done intentionally; we have injured no man's reputation, character, person or property; we were uniting together to preserve ourselves, our wives and our children from utter degradation and starvation. We challenge any man to prove that this is not the case.

Lord John Russell (1792–1878)

John Russell, the son of the Duke of Bedford, became an MP in 1813 at the age of 21.

During the 1820s he campaigned to allow Roman Catholics to vote (at this time the vote was restricted to a number of wealthy men – Catholics, women and most ordinary working men were not allowed to vote in a General Election!) and helped draw up the 1832 Reform Bill which extended the vote.

He was Prime Minister in 1846–52 and 1865–6 and during these times helped pass laws limiting working hours in factories and setting up a public health system.

Landlords

Most of the land in Ireland was owned by landlords who lived in England. They rarely, if ever, visited their estates. Some landlords did live in Ireland but, instead of investing money in their land, spent it on good living in Dublin. A few landlords tried to do their best for their tenants. But tenants could only afford low rents, and this did not bring in enough money for landlords to improve the land.

Population and land

Between 1821 and 1841 the population of Ireland increased from 6.8 million to 8.2 million. There was enormous competition for land. Tenant farmers, who rented their land from the landowners, **sub-let** to more and more labourers. Hundreds of families tried to live off plots of land which were too small to make a profit; they just about supported the family – if they were lucky.

Crops

Most Irish people lived on unimproved land which was wet and soggy. There they grew the only crop they could – the potato. And they lived on it. A diet of milk and potatoes was enough to keep them healthy, provided the crop was good. There were areas of more fertile land where corn was grown, but the corn was for selling, not eating. Without this income the Irish people could not pay the rent.

Famine!

In the spring of 1845 a deadly virus spread among the growing potatoes. When they were dug up, one in three was diseased by **blight**. Famine was a very real possibility for the 4 million people who depended on potatoes to live. The corn survived, but if the tenants did not pay the rent, they would be **evicted**. So it was best to go hungry and sell the corn. Boat load after boat load of corn sailed off to be sold in England. Everything depended on the next year's potato crop.

Source A

From *The Condition of the Working Class in England* by F. Engels, 1844. Despite the title, he is writing about the Irish in Ireland.

They have potatoes half enough for thirty weeks in the year, and the rest nothing. When the time comes in the spring when this food reaches its end, wife and children go to beg. Meanwhile the husband goes in search of work either in Ireland or England, and returns at the potato harvest to his family. This is the condition in which nine-tenths of the Irish country folks live.

This engraving shows how Irish labourers lived before the Famine.

Source B

Many people had been forced to eat their **seed potatoes**, but even so there were enough to plant about two-thirds of the normal quantity. But many diseased tubers had been planted and the spring was mild and damp. Blight spread again. Field after field turned black with rotting potatoes. The entire crop failed. The threat of famine had become a reality.

Disease

With famine came disease. When people are starving, ordinary diseases, like 'flu and measles, become killers. Scurvy was common. When people have scurvy their teeth drop out and their legs turn black because of burst blood vessels. The most serious disease of all was typhus. Typhus victims have a high fever, rashes and sores, swollen, blackened faces – and they smell awful. The Irish called typhus 'famine fever' and most people abandoned anyone who caught it. In 1846 typhus reached **epidemic** proportions. About one million Irish died in the Famine. Almost 90% of them died not from starvation but from disease.

Source C

Written by a magistrate from Cork who visited Skibbereen in west Cork in December 1846:

I entered some of the hovels. In the first, six famished and ghastly skeletons, to all appearance dead, were huddled in a corner on some filthy straw, their only covering what seemed a ragged horse-cloth. I approached in horror and found by a low moaning that they were alive, they were in fever – four children, a woman and what had once been a man.

An Irish funeral during the Famine.

Source D

Potato Blight

The fungus, which ruined the Irish potato crop, is *Phytophthora infestans*. This fungus attacks the leaves of the plant. It drains them of sap and so they turn black and die. The fungus multiplies quickly in warm, wet weather because it produces spores, which are carried on the wind to other plants. If the fungus comes early in the season and the leaves wither and die, the potato tubers will not form properly. If it comes late, the spores are washed into the ground and attack the tubers, which quickly turn black and rot.

Potato blight still exists in the world today. The new strains are more virulent than those which destroyed the Irish potato crop in the 1840s. In 1980, 30% of the Polish potato crop was destroyed by blight. During 1991–5, the USA had its worst years of potato production because of blight. Blight attacked potato crops as far afield as Siberia and Mexico. Blight can be controlled chemically, but scientists are trying to develop environmentally friendly methods of control as well as blight-resistance potatoes.

Since Ireland was part of the United Kingdom, people expected the British government to provide a solution to the problem of famine.

Relief Committees

Each district in Ireland had a Relief Committee of poor-law guardians, clergymen, teachers and magistrates, both Catholic and Protestant. Their job was to do their best to see people had the help they needed.

Cheap maize

The government spent £100,000 on maize from the USA. It was shipped to huge **depots** in Limerick and Cork and then distributed to smaller ones around the country. There were two main problems. Firstly, there were some parts of Ireland where these government depots were the only source of food, and they were besieged by starving people. Secondly, the maize was very difficult to grind into flour; Irish people had never cooked maize or eaten it before, so they made it into a kind of porridge. They hated it and called it 'Peel's **Brimstone**' because it was bright yellow and Robert Peel was the Prime Minister responsible for ordering the supply of cheap maize. But the Irish ate 'Peel's Brimstone'. They had no choice.

Public works

The government organised hundreds of road-building schemes so that starving people could work and earn money. Ireland didn't actually need the roads; Ireland needed land improvement schemes so that food could be grown. But the government wouldn't fund these because to do so would have meant using public money to benefit private landowners. By February 1847, 700,000 people were employed in road-making. This was costing a great deal and the government stopped all such schemes by June 1847.

Emigration

Another, more terrible 'solution' was found. By the time of the third year of famine, 1848, government help and sympathy were running thin. Irish landlords were forced to do what they could. They were themselves facing ruin. Their tenants had paid no rent for years. They couldn't improve their land and they couldn't make any profit from it. So they set about clearing tenants off their land and letting it in larger parcels to people who could pay.

Where were the poverty-stricken tenants to go? Some simply starved. Others decided to try their luck overseas. How did they pay for their passage? The cost of a passage was roughly the same as the cost of keeping a pauper in the workhouse for six months. So many poor law guardians and landlords paid the fares of families willing to go to the USA or Canada. It was cheaper that way. Others had their passage paid for by various charitable committees set up in Ireland and England.

Source A

Many ordinary people in England did what they could to help. Some formed committees and knitted, sewed and held fêtes to raise money for the starving Irish. Some, like this Quaker, William Bennett, went to Ireland with bales of clothes and sacks of turnip and flax seed to give away. Here he writes about the effect of soup kitchens. Usually they didn't serve soup at all, but a thick porridge called 'stirabout' made from maize flour or oatmeal.

At Tencurry and Turbid 3200 quarts (3635 litres) of porridge were distributed daily, to upwards of 800 families, one of the boilers being filled four or five times. The amount of distress ended in this way is impossible to calculate, and was seen in the improved appearance of the poor people since the soup kitchens had been in action.

By 1851 about one million Irish people had died from starvation and disease and another million had emigrated. Half the population of Ireland simply wasn't there any more.

In 1848 the British Parliament gave money to Irish **workhouses** and supplied them with cheap maize. In this picture, starving people are besieging an Irish workhouse, desperately trying to get food.

Source C

Sir William Butler, an Irish soldier and author, described what he had seen as a boy.

One day I was taken by my father to the scene of an eviction. On one side of the road was a ruined church; on the other side stood some dozen houses which were to be pulled down. At a signal from the sheriff the work began. The miserable inmates were dragged out upon the road; the thatched roofs were torn down and the earthen walls battered in by crowbars; the screaming women, the half-naked children, the paralysed grandmother and the tottering grandfather were hauled out. I was twelve years old at that time; but I think if a loaded gun had been put into my hands I would have fired into that crowd of villains as they plied their horrid trade by the ruined church of Tampul-da-voun.

Sir Robert Peel (1788–1850)

Robert Peel was a Tory politician who was Prime Minister twice, during 1834–5 and 1841–6. He first became an MP in 1809 when he represented Cashel, in Ireland. As Chief Secretary for Ireland (1812–18) he was fiercely anti-Catholic, and was nick-named 'Orange Peel' because he supported the Protestants. By 1829 he had changed his mind. He supported the Catholic Emancipation Bill, which was intended to give Catholics in Ireland the same rights as Protestants. The Irish Famine convinced Peel that the Corn Laws, which kept the price of grain artificially high, had to end. He pushed their repeal through Parliament in 1846, but this split the Tory party and ended his own career.

In the period covered by this book there was a major change in the way that Britain earned its living. In the mid-eighteenth century Britain was still an agricultural country. Most of its six million inhabitants lived in villages or small towns and earned their living working on the land. By modern standards there was only one town of any size, London, with a population of over half a million. Britain's major industry was the making of woollen cloth. But this did not generally happen in factories. Instead, spinning and weaving were done in the home under what historians have called the Domestic System.

Changes through power

There were some small factories in eighteenth-century Britain, though the lack of a reliable source of power meant that they had to rely on water-wheels to turn their machines. But at the beginning of the century one invention led to such dramatic changes in the way goods were produced that we now talk of an 'Industrial Revolution'. In 1698 steam was used to drive a pump to remove water from tin mines in Cornwall. In the next hundred years improvements to this 'steam engine' meant that it could be used to drive machinery in a factory. Now that there was a reliable source of power, factories sprang up and Britain began its Industrial Revolution. The factories, however, were mostly in the north of England, where coalfields provided fuel for the steam engines.

Source A

A steam engine built in 1778. Note how a series of cogs attached to the drive rod enable the engine to drive a wheel (see page 37). This was the basis on which trains were later to work.

Source B

Hebburn Colliery, County Durham, in 1844.

An engraving of a textile mill in Derby.

More factories meant more coal had to be produced to power the steam engines. Iron production had to increase to provide the materials for building steam engines and factories. The factories needed workers and so houses were built for them to live in. Soon towns with factories, or close to coalfields, began to develop into modern cities. Of course, people who lived in cities and worked in factories could not grow their own food, so farming had to change to produce more food for those who were unable to grow their own.

Workshop of the World

The Industrial Revolution led to Britain becoming the 'Workshop of the World', but this could not have happened without developments in transport. Raw materials had to reach factories, finished goods had to be transported to ports or markets in Britain, and food had to get to the cities. The rut-infested roads of eighteenth-century Britain could not do this – but the new canals, and later the railways, proved ideal!

Isambard Kingdom Brunel (1806–59)

Brunel was one of Britain's most famous engineers. He designed the Clifton Bridge across the Avon Gorge at Bristol and built much of the Great Western Railway from London to Bristol.

He later turned to designing steamships. He built the *Great Western* in 1838 and the first iron-hulled ship, the *Great Britain* in 1843. In 1858 he launched the huge Great Eastern, which for the next 40 years was the largest ship in the world.

Source D

A painting from 1788 showing the country's first iron bridge. During the Industrial Revolution, iron manufacturers found a way to use coal-fired furnaces to produce good-quality iron from which bridges could be built.

At the beginning of the eighteenth century more than half the population of England worked on the land or in a trade, such as milling, that was connected with agriculture. Most of the land was owned by rich **aristocrats** or gentry who rented it out to tenant farmers. These farmers paid labourers to work for them.

Strip farming

In much of England, farming used the 'open field' system, which involved dividing a village's fields into strips with every farmer having strips in each field. Every four years one of the village's fields was left fallow. That meant nothing was grown in it. Instead it was left to recover. As well as the fields which were cultivated there was also common land on which all villagers had the right to graze their livestock.

From the beginning of the eighteenth century, the population began to grow rapidly and more food was needed. This caused food prices to rise. Some farmers began to look at ways of growing more food and making more money.

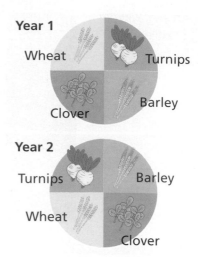

Year 1 — Wheat, Turnips, Clover, Barley

Year 2 — Turnips, Barley, Wheat, Clover

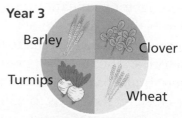

Year 3 — Barley, Clover, Turnips, Wheat

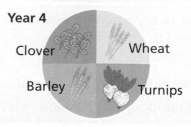

Year 4 — Clover, Wheat, Barley, Turnips

The Norfolk Rotation System ➤
Each crop extracts different nutrients from the soil, so they can be grown one after the other each year. Livestock can be put in the field of clover. As they eat, they also manure the fields.

Source A

A painting called *The Haymakers* by George Stubbs. It was painted in 1786.

Source B

From a report called *Sanitary Conditions of the Labouring Population of Great Britain*, 1842.

Most of the cottages are of the worst kind; some are mud hovels with piles of filth close to the doors. The mud floors of many are much below the level of the road and in wet seasons are little better than clay. Persons living in such cottages are generally very poor, very dirty and usually in rags, living almost wholly on bread and potatoes.

Enclosure

One way was to 'enclose' land – putting hedges round fields and farming them as one unit instead of in strips. As wealthy landowners began to enclose more and more land, they were able to use more efficient farming methods and needed fewer labourers. Some unscrupulous landowners also enclosed common land, so the ordinary farm labourers were doubly hit. Now they had nowhere to graze their own animals.

Farming techniques

Enclosure led to improvements in farming techniques. In Norfolk, a system of rotating crops, so that there was no need to rest the land for a year, helped boost production. This was also a time when new machinery began to be introduced into farming. A seed drill was invented to sow seed under the soil, ploughs became lighter so they were easier to use, and machines were used for separating the wheat from the **chaff**. This 'threshing' had previously been done by hand.

With enclosed fields, animals could be kept apart. This meant that not only were weak or diseased animals kept away from others, but farmers could select which animals to breed from. This selective breeding led to a vast increase in the size of livestock as farmers began breeding animals with shorter legs and larger bodies for more meat.

More efficient

The changes in agriculture brought great profits for landowners and farming became much more efficient. But many labourers lost their jobs, and there were periods when even the great landowners found it hard to make money from farming. As transport improved and refrigeration and canning were introduced, farmers also faced competition from abroad. This competition, together with a run of wet summers, led to terrible hardships in the 1870s. British farming had to become even more efficient before it could provide enough food at a cheap price for the country's industrial workers.

Charles Townshend (1675–1738)

Charles Townshend succeeded his father as Viscount Townshend in 1687. He was a very important statesman in the reign of George I.

Townshend was educated at Eton College and Cambridge University before entering politics. He played a major part in bringing George I to the throne after Queen Anne's death in 1714 and in defeating the Jacobite rebellion of 1715. However, his interest in improving agricultural methods has led to him becoming known as 'Turnip Townshend'.

1710		1795
370 lb	Cattle	800 lb
70 lb	Calves	140 lb
28 lb	Sheep	80 lb
18 lb	Lambs	50 lb

Average weight of livestock at Smithfield market in 1710 and 1795.

THOMAS TURNER

Thomas Turner lived for most of his life in the Sussex village of East Hoathly. He was the village shopkeeper there – and very much more! We know the details of about eleven years of his life (1754–65) because he kept a diary. This tells us a lot, not only about Thomas' life, but about life in general in a small village in eighteenth-century England.

As you read these extracts from Thomas Turner's diary (in *italics*) and look at the other sources, work out what they tell you about Thomas Turner himself and what they tell you about life in his village and in eighteenth-century England.

Important dates in Thomas Turner's life

9 June 1729	Born at Groombridge, Kent.
June 1735	Family moved to Framfield, Sussex, where Thomas' father ran the village shop.
1750	Thomas rented a shop in East Hoathly, Sussex.
May 1752	Thomas' father died.
15 Oct 1753	Thomas married 20-year-old Peggy Slater. Their one child, a boy, died aged five months.
1 April 1759	Thomas' mother died.
23 June 1761	Thomas' wife died.
31 July 1765	Thomas married his second wife – Molly Hicks. They had one daughter and six sons, two of whom died when they were babies.
1766	Thomas bought his shop at East Hoathly, Sussex.
6 Feb 1793	Thomas Turner died and was buried in East Hoathley churchyard.

Shopkeeper

Mon 7 July 1755
Paid Halland the gardener 17 pence in full for cucumbers I sold for him.

Wed 24 Dec 1755
Paid John Jenner 21 shillings in payment for hats received from him today. In the evening wrote out Peter Adam's bill amounting to £8 16 shillings 1 pence. Gave 2 oz tobacco for two cheeses from Lewes.

Wed 1 Aug 1759
After breakfast rode over to Framfield and stayed there while my brother went to Uckfield to get me a pound of green tea, for which I paid him 9 shillings 3 pence.

Looking after the dead

Sat 8 March 1755
At the funeral of Mrs Piper. Gave out 20 pairs of men's and women's gloves.

Sat 27 Dec 1761
I set out for Lewes in order to get brass plates for Mr Calverley's coffin.

Sun 28 Dec 1761
In the morn I walked down to Whyly with a shroud, sheet etc. for Mr Calverley.

Teaching children

Thurs 13 Mar 1755
Mr Miller promised me his son should come to me to be taught.

Fri 20 June 1755
This day being my birthday I treated my scholars to about five quarts of strong beer.

Tues 17 June 1760
In the afternoon kept the school for Mr Long, he going to a cricket match at Chiddingly.

Helping the poor

Mon 22 Dec 1755

It being St Thomas' Day I gave to the poor of the parish, being about 30 in number, each one penny and a drink of beer.

Collecting taxes

Fri 9 Jan 1761

After breakfast went to Maresfield to meet the receiver-general of the land-tax, where I paid his clerk, Mr Thomas Gerry, the sum of £62 for half a year's land tax due from this parish.

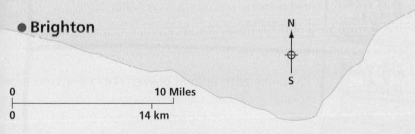

Groombridge

SUSSEX

Uckfield ● **Framfield**

● **East Hoathly**
● **Chiddingly**

● **Lewes**

● **Brighton**

N

S

| 0 | | 10 Miles |
| 0 | | 14 km |

Having fun

Thurs 27 May 1756

My wife and I went to Dicker Fair. We met with Miss Day and several more and I took them to a booth to treat them to a drink. I spent three shillings.

Sun 25 Dec 1757

This being Christmas Day the widow Marchant, Hannah Marchant and James Marchant dined with us on a buttock of boiled beef, a plum suet pudding and a pearl barley pudding, turnips and a wild plum pie.

Thurs 23 Feb 1758

During a wild party some of my friends poured into my room and made me put on my wife's petticoat. They made me dance with them without shoes or stockings until they had emptied their bottle of wine.

Source A

A modern photograph of Thomas Turner's cottage in East Hoathly.

Before steam

Before the development of steam power there were four main types of power used. None of them was totally satisfactory, as the cartoon below shows. Unreliable power sources meant factory owners could not always produce their goods. This in turn caused them to lose money. A more reliable form of power had to be found if the Industrial Revolution was to progress further. Steam was the answer.

The first British steam engine was developed in 1698 by Thomas Savery, who created the machine to pump water out of Cornish mines. However, it couldn't raise water above 20m, and was unreliable. It was dangerous, too, since the boilers were weak and often exploded. Little surprise, then, that it was replaced 14 years later by a much more effective machine, developed by Thomas Newcomen.

Thomas Newcomen

Newcomen grew up in Devon and knew the problems of the Cornish mines. He set about producing a better steam engine that could pump water up from 50m. However, this engine relied on a lot of coal, and there were no coalmines in Cornwall, so it was very expensive to run.

James Watt

In 1769, 40 years after Newcomen's death, James Watt was asked by the University of Glasgow to repair a model Newcomen engine. Whilst working on it, Watt became aware of how fuel-hungry the engine was. So he set about finding ways to improve the engine to produce more power without using so much coal.

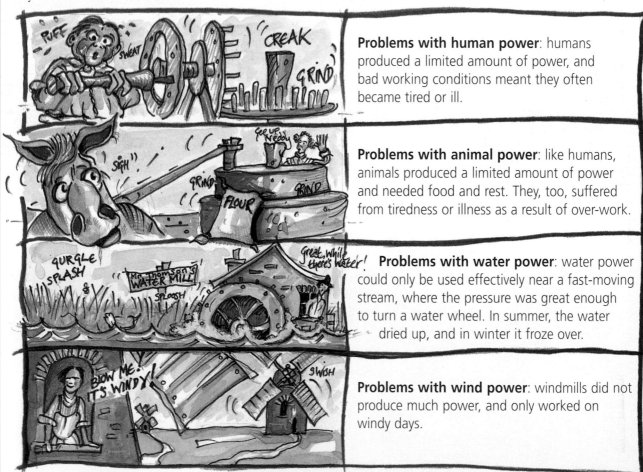

Problems with human power: humans produced a limited amount of power, and bad working conditions meant they often became tired or ill.

Problems with animal power: like humans, animals produced a limited amount of power and needed food and rest. They, too, suffered from tiredness or illness as a result of over-work.

Problems with water power: water power could only be used effectively near a fast-moving stream, where the pressure was great enough to turn a water wheel. In summer, the water dried up, and in winter it froze over.

Problems with wind power: windmills did not produce much power, and only worked on windy days.

Watt was so successful that his improved engine used only a quarter of the fuel needed by Newcomen's engine. Now factory owners began to look at the possibility of using the steam engine to drive their machines.

By 1776 Watt's first engine was being used in collieries. By now Watt had joined forces with Matthew Boulton, and they set about making a steam engine that could work in rotary motion, instead of just parallel (see below). This was achieved in 1781, and opened up many other industries to the reliability of steam power. It is not hard to see why the steam engine was one of the key developments of the Industrial Revolution.

By 1800 the industries that relied on steam power were wide and varied – from brewing to coin making, mining to sugar making. The cheap and reliable power produced by the new steam engines helped make Britain the most important manufacturing country in the world.

Source A

The writer James Boswell visited Boulton and Watt's factory in Soho. Boswell wrote this after the visit.

I shall never forget Mr Boulton's expression to me: 'I sell here, Sir, what all the world desires to have – power.'

This is a diagram of a typical 'sun and planet gear'. The driving rod (A) goes up and down (parallel motion), powered by the steam engine. At the end of the rod is a cog (B), which has teeth that slot into another cog in the middle of the wheel (C). As the teeth in the two cogs connect, the wheel is forced round, creating rotary motion.

Source B

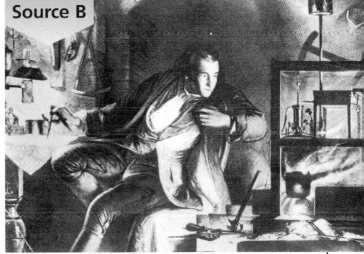

James Watt, painted in 1869.

James Watt (1736–1819)

Watt was a Scottish engineer who is famous for developing the steam engine. He did improve existing models and, along with Matthew Boulton, produced the first really effective engines.

2.5 LIVING AND WORKING CONDITIONS IN INDUSTRIAL BRITAIN

An increasing population

During the eighteenth and nineteenth centuries the population of Britain increased dramatically. From 1801 the government began to take a census (count) of the population every ten years, and from 1837 official records of births, marriages and deaths were kept. For the years before 1801 historians have had to make guesses about the population based on how many people were paying tax or how many were recorded in church parish registers as being baptised or buried.

What we can be sure of, however, is that the number of people in the country increased. By 1900 there were more than six times as many people living in Britain as there had been in 1750.

Historians are not really very sure about why this population increase happened. Obviously if more people are born than die, the population will increase. During the eighteenth century, the average age at which people married dropped from 27 to nearer 20, so families tended to be larger. As jobs for children became available in the new factories, people were less concerned about not being able to feed their families, so this may have helped too.

Inoculation

In the eighteenth century a method of fighting the killer disease, smallpox, was introduced into Britain. This treatment was developed by Edward Jenner (1749–1823). He noted that dairymaids who caught cowpox from cows never caught smallpox. He inoculated a child with cowpox, Then a few months later with smallpox and the child failed to develop the disease. Having fought off the mild disease cowpox, the child's body was ready to fight if infected by the more severe smallpox germs.

Source A

LONDON going out of Town. — or — The March of Bricks & Mortar!

A cartoon published in 1829 called 'The March of Bricks and Mortar'.

Of course, if families have more children, there are more people to have children in future and so the population keeps increasing.

The death rate may also have decreased during this time. Although many families lived in appalling conditions in the new industrial towns, there were big improvements in medical care, particularly with the introduction of **inoculation** against killer diseases such as smallpox. Many families were also eating better food and more of it, as improvements in agriculture and transport made food cheaper and more readily available. We should not imagine, however, that life was constantly improving for everyone. There were still many examples of families being short of food through low wages, unemployment, illness or old age.

Where did all the extra people live?

During the eighteenth century there was a major change in the pattern of population in Britain. Before the Industrial Revolution, the vast majority of people lived in the countryside and their lives revolved around farming. With the invention of an efficient steam engine and the growth of factories, people began to move into towns to work in the newly mechanised industries. It was during this period that many of our modern cities, such as Birmingham, Leeds and Manchester, the centre of the cotton industry, began to develop.

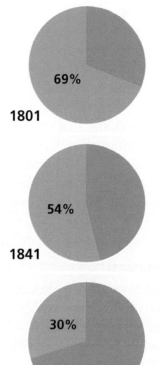

Percentage of population living in the countryside

69% — 1801

54% — 1841

30% — 1901

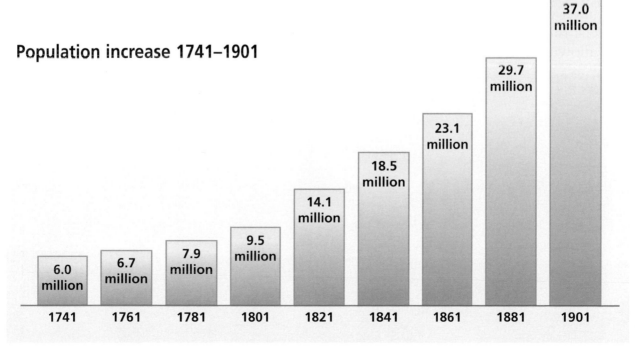

Population increase 1741–1901

1741	1761	1781	1801	1821	1841	1861	1881	1901
6.0 million	6.7 million	7.9 million	9.5 million	14.1 million	18.5 million	23.1 million	29.7 million	37.0 million

Problems in the towns

The influx of people into the growing industrial towns produced a steady supply of workers for the new factories, but it also produced a number of problems.

Housing

As workers moved into towns, the factory owners built houses for them to live in. There were no planning regulations for the factory owners to follow, so they could build whatever kinds of house they wanted. Obviously, factory owners wanted to provide reasonable housing for their workers, but they did not want to spend more money than they had to. Buying land cost money, so it was important to build as many houses as possible on each piece of land. This meant that houses were built back-to-back in long rows. There were no gardens and very few windows. Rooms were small and since families were usually large, conditions were very cramped.

Sanitation

Very few workers' houses had running water, so people had to fetch their water from a pipe at the end of the street. There were also no toilets. It was not uncommon for whole streets to share one toilet. Can you imagine what it must have been like for 200–300 people to share one toilet? Of course, this toilet would not be an efficient flushing toilet like today. Instead the 'privy' would be a wooden seat over a hole called a 'cess pit'. From time to time, men were employed to empty the cess pits with buckets. But the job was so unpleasant that they were only allowed to work at night!

The city of Manchester in 1850.

Source C

Average age of death in 1840 in four English industrial towns. One of the reasons the ages are so low is because so many babies and children died before reaching adulthood.

	Labourers	Gentry
Bolton	18 years	34 years
Leeds	19 years	44 years
Liverpool	15 years	35 years
Manchester	17 years	38 years

A terraced street in London in 1872.

Source D

The Earl of Shaftesbury (1801–85)

Anthony Ashley Cooper became the seventh Earl of Shaftesbury in 1851. He was educated at Harrow public school and Oxford University. He first became an MP when he was elected for Woodstock in 1826.

He had a passionate belief in improving living and working conditions for the poor. He helped introduce laws to improve factory conditions, prohibit the employment of women and children in mines, and establish a maximum ten hour day for factory workers.

Source E

An account of the state of the River Aire, a main source of drinking water for the city of Leeds, written in 1841:

Into the river flow the contents of about 200 water closets [toilets] and similar places, a great number of common drains, the draining from dunghills, the Infirmary (dead leeches, poultices from patients, etc.), slaughter houses, chemical soap, gas, dung, dyehouses and factories, pig manure and all sorts of decomposed animal and vegetable substances.

This amounts to about 30 million gallons (150 million litres) per year of filth flowing into the river between Armley Mills and the Kings Mill.

Source F

An extract from a report on the town of Greenock in 1844:

In one part of the town there is a dunghill with a hundred cubic yards of filth collected from all parts of the town. It belongs to a person who deals in dung; he sells it by the cartful. To please his customers he keeps it for some time before selling it. The heap is enclosed by a wall twelve feet high, but comes over the top of the wall. The filthy liquid oozes through the wall and runs over the pavement. There is a housing estate nearby and all food and drink must be covered; if it is left for a minute, the flies attack it and make it unfit for use, from the strong taste of the dunghill left by flies.

Cholera arrives!

In early 1830 word arrived in Britain of a new disease which had started in India and was sweeping across Europe. The disease was cholera. More than half of those who caught it died a very painful death. It was spread through water which had been contaminated by the faeces of those who already had the disease.

At that time people had little idea what caused cholera, but they soon found out how deadly it could be. The first case of the new disease occurred in Sunderland in late October 1831. The government ordered that the port of Sunderland should be closed but this did not stop the spread of the disease. Soon it was spreading across Britain and killed over 50,000 people. There were further outbreaks in 1848, 1854 and 1866.

Source G

A report in a local newspaper in Sunderland in early October 1831 – a few weeks before the outbreak of cholera in the town.

The following are the symptoms of the disease: giddiness, sick stomach, slow or weak pulse, cramp at the top of the fingers and toes. This is followed by vomiting and diarrhoea. The face becomes sharp and shrunken, the eyes sink and look wild, the lips, face, neck, hands and feet turn blue, purple, and black. The skin is deadly cold and often damp.

In the treatment of this disease no specific remedy has yet been discovered, nor has any cure been successful. But the greatest confidence can be expressed in the doctors of this country who will surely find a way to treat the disease.

How cholera spread from India to England.

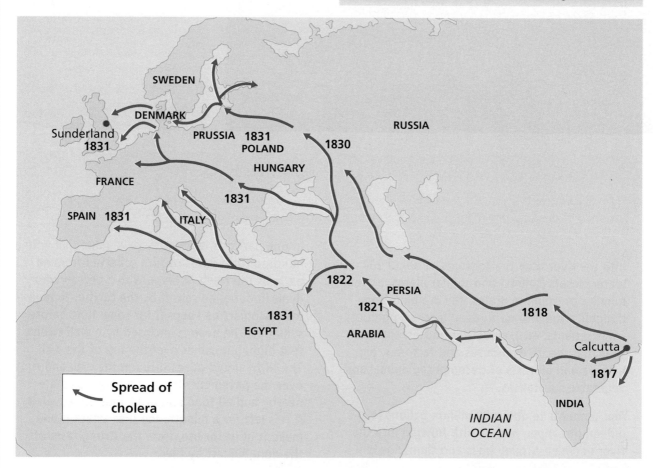

Source H

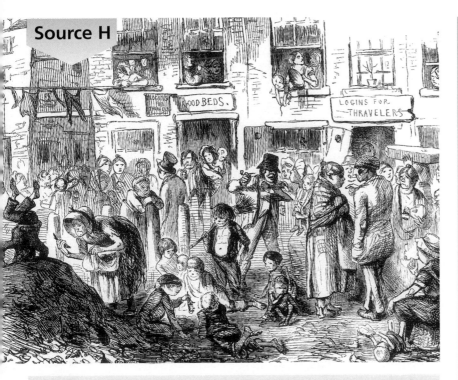

A Court for King Cholera – a cartoon from the time, showing the dreadful conditions in which some people lived.

Lord Londonderry (1778–1854)

Charles William Stewart, the third Marquis of Londonderry, had a very distinguished military and political career.

He entered the army in 1794 and became a general by 1810, though his military career was hampered by severe battle wounds in 1813.

He also served as under-secretary of war and became a privy councillor in 1814. In 1819 he married into the wealthy Vane family.

During his colourful life, Londonderry also fought a duel and was a coffin bearer at Wellington's funeral.

Source I

An extract from a letter written to Lord Londonderry, by his doctor, J. Brown. Lord Londonderry was a Sunderland mine owner who could not export his coal from Sunderland because of government restrictions. On 13 November Lord Londonderry wrote to a London newspaper complaining about the restrictions and quoting Dr Brown.

My Lord,

After careful observation I have come to the following conclusions:

1. **That cholera has not come to England from abroad.**
2. **That the disease is subsiding.**
3. **That the disease occurs most amongst the poor who live in the worst conditions and are already weak through previous diseases and too much alcohol.**
4. **The restrictions placed on trade are unnecessary because the disease is not infectious.**

Your Lordship's Obedient Servant,

Dr J. Brown

Source J

Part of the report into conditions in Leeds published in the *Sanitary Conditions of the Labouring Population of Great Britain* in 1842:

By the inspection of the map which has been prepared at my request to show where the disease has broken out, I can see that it is most common in the uncleansed and close streets occupied by the labouring poor. In the badly cleansed and badly drained areas the number of deaths is almost twice that of the areas with better conditions.

Dark, satanic mills?

The invention of a reliable form of power (steam) and the development of impressive new machinery meant that the Domestic System gradually died out and was replaced by the Factory System. From now on, industrial workers would come to the factory instead of working from home.

One of the first industries affected by this change was textile manufacture. Early inventors such as Richard Arkwright had developed machines which were too big to be used in the home and so were set up in factories using water for power. One such factory was the famous Cromford Mill in Derbyshire. However, later inventions, such as Cartwright's Power Loom, needed steam to be effective. By the early years of the nineteenth century, both cotton and wool manufacture were becoming dominated by factories using steam for power.

Working conditions

The purpose of the factories was to make money. This was done by making employees work for as long as possible and paying low wages. Inside the factories, conditions were poor. Cotton manufacture required high temperatures to prevent the thread snapping and, of course, the steam engines also made factories hot. Dangerous machinery was not fenced off and there were no safety regulations.

Source K

TO
Journeymen Spinners
Wanted Immediately,
From Eighty to One Hundred
MULE SPINNERS,

For a New Mill and other Mills, in Great Bolton, which New Mill is complete with new Machinery now ready gaited, and will commence running on Monday Morning next, adjoining to which Mills are a Number of Cottages, for the convenience and accommodation of Spinners: liberal Wages will be given and constant employ.

For further particulars apply to Messrs. ORMROD and HARDCASTLE, of Bolton aforesaid, Cotton Spinners.

An advertisement for spinners to work in a new mill in Bolton in 1816.

Source M

A picture of children working in a textile factory. This picture comes from a novel written in 1840, giving an account of the sad life of an orphan boy.

Source L

A selection of fines for workers at a cotton mill near Manchester in 1823.

Having a window open	1 shilling
Whistling	1 shilling
Dirty at work	1 shilling
Being five minutes late	1 shilling
Being sick and not sending a replacement	6 shillings

Laws to improve working conditions

Factory Act 1819: Children to work no more than 12 hours a day

Factory Act 1833: Children under 9 not to work in textile mills. 10–13-year-olds limited to 48 hours' work a week

Factory Act 1844: Women limited to 12 hours' work a day

Factory Act 1847: Women and children limited to 10 hours' work a day

Factory Act 1850: Women's and children's work limit increased to 10.5 hours but must be between 6 a.m. and 6 p.m.

Factory Act 1874: No worker to work more than 56.5 hours per week

Robert Owen (1771–1858)

Owen was the owner of a factory in New Lanark, Scotland, where conditions for workers were considerably better than in most factories.

Owen was apprenticed to a draper at the age of nine and learned about the textile business. He became manager in a factory at the age of 20 and in 1799 bought his own factory at New Lanark. He believed that better working conditions led to greater productivity. He refused to employ young children, provided education for the older ones and limited the hours of adults. In 1825 he bought land in America and set up a village where his ideas of equality could be put into practice. The scheme failed and cost Owen 80% of his personal fortune!

Punishments were very harsh in the factories. Fines were common and 'overseers' were employed to check that work was being done properly. If not, corporal punishment was often used to encourage better work. Children were employed in the factories from a very early age and often had the job of 'scavenging' under the machines to pick up waste cotton or wool. The use of machines meant that women and children could do most of the work, since little muscle power was needed.

Cruel?

There have been criticisms of the conditions in factories and most employers have been portrayed as cruel. However, we must consider things from the perspective of people at the time. Workers coming into factories from agricultural work were used to working very long hours in difficult conditions. They were also used to their children working. In many families the children's wages were vital to life. But agricultural workers were not used to working to the clock. Being five minutes late meant nothing in a field, but cost the employer money in wasted steam in a factory. To train workers to be punctual, employers sometimes had to use harsh punishments.

Some factory owners, such as Robert Owen, treated their workers better than most owners did. There were also large numbers of **reformers** who campaigned for change and helped get laws passed to improve conditions. But we must be careful not to let factory owners off too lightly!

Source N

An account of a day in the life of a mill girl, written by William Dodd, a factory reformer, in 1842.

Too poor to own a clock, her family pays a watchman to tap on the window at 4.30 each morning. After she drinks coffee and eats bread, the mill bell warns her to hurry. At 5.30 work begins. Two hours later the pace of the machines slackens enough to allow her to clean off the dust and have breakfast – if she is quick. At noon the machines stop and she cleans them thoroughly before rushing home for soup and bread. She is back in place by one o'clock and works until seven. After cleaning her machines again, she returns home fourteen hours after setting off. This is six days a week (though she may get home early on a Sunday).

Source A

| Registration District | City of London |

1842. Marriage solemnized at 106 Shoe Lane in the of West London in the City of London

No.	When married	Name and surname	Age	Condition	Rank or profession	Residence at the time of marriage	Father's name and surname	Rank or profession of father
1	September 28th	George Woolf	Full	Bachelor	Accountant	106 Shoe Lane	Joseph Woolf	
		Maria Mordecai		Spinster		20 John Street Waterloo Road	Jonas Mordecai	

Married in the Congregation of the New Synagogue according to the Rites & Ceremonies of the German & Polish Jews by me

This marriage was solemnized between us, George Woolf / Maria Woolf

In the presence of us, P Harris / Moses Levy

Abm Barrett Reader / J L Lindenthal Registrar

A detail from the marriage certificate of George Woolf and Maria Mordecai, September 1842.

Maria Mordecai and George Woolf were married on 28 September 1842 in George's home, 106 Shoe Lane, London. Maria and George were Jews whose families had fled from persecution in central Europe in the eighteenth century. The wedding was attended by George's brothers and sisters, Sophia, Hannah, Julia, Elizabeth, Fanny, Samuel and Philip, together with his father Joseph and mother Alcry. We know that Maria's father, Jonas, was also present but we do not know which other relatives were there.

Cholera

On 18 April 1844 Maria gave birth to a son, who was named Joseph after his grandfather. In 1849 Maria became pregnant once more. But in June disaster struck the Woolf family. Cholera! Their home in Shoe Lane was in a row of tall, dark houses which rarely saw sunlight. The inhabitants drew their water from the nearby Fleet Brook. This was the same brook into which household waste from the streets would have gone. It was a perfect breeding ground for cholera.

Source B

This drawing of George Woolf was made in 1858 from an earlier, lost portrait.

Source C

Joseph Woolf, the son of George and Maria, drawn in 1858.

No.	When and where died	Name and surname	Sex	Age	Occupation	Cause of death	Signature, description, and residence of informant	When registered	Signature of registrar

REGISTRATION DISTRICT — *West London*

1849. DEATH in the Sub-district of *West London* in the *City of London*

| 100 | Eighteenth June 1849 106 Shoe Lane St. Brides | Maria Woolf | Female | 32 years. | Wife of George Woolf Accountant. | Diarrhoea 8 days Cholera 4 days Premature Labour 32 hours Exhaustion Certified. | G. Woolf Present at the Death 106 Shoe Lane London. | Nineteenth June 1849 | William Nason Registrar |

A detail from the death certificate of Maria Woolf, June 1849.

Death

A cholera epidemic hit Britain in 1848–9 and 62,000 people died. No one knew how it spread. Maria, seven months pregnant, caught the disease. The people with her would have tried desperately to keep her cool by sponging her down and giving her water to drink. The water, however, would have come from the Fleet Brook. Within eight days both Maria and her premature baby were dead.

George and his son Joseph survived the cholera epidemic. George died two years later from tuberculosis. Joseph was brought up by his Aunt Julia and Uncle Joel. He died in 1911 having worked all his life as a furniture upholsterer.

Source F

Kate Vaughan-Williams, a modern doctor, said this about Maria Woolf's death.

Maria probably had cholera for eight days, from when the diarrhoea first started. She would have had acute pain in her abdomen; smelly, explosive, watery diarrhoea and a high fever. All this would have triggered off early labour. A long labour like that would increase risk of infection. She was probably bleeding heavily, too. Eventually her circulatory system would have collapsed and then she died.

Source E

A mourning ring, made after Maria Woolf's death. It contains woven strands of Maria's hair. The ring would have been worn by her husband, or another relative, in memory of Maria.

Jacob's Island, 1849

In the space of three months in 1849 more than 6,000 people died of cholera in a small area of London on the south bank of the River Thames. This area, known as 'Jacob's Island', was described at the time as being 'bounded to the north and east by filth and fear, and to the south and west by squalor, rags and disease.'

The houses on Jacob's Island hung out over the river, so that the people in them slept directly over the foul smelling water. Most of the houses had their own pig sties and many people also kept ducks and chickens. All this animal waste, added to the human waste, made it no wonder cholera spread so rapidly in this area.

Source A

Bradford in the 1840s.

The first factory, a mill that spun wool, was built in 1803. By 1840 over thirty more spinning mills had been built and the population had grown from around 13,000 to about 67,000. Bradford mills specialised in making worsted.

Woolcombing at home

Woolcombing was a filthy job. In Bradford the woolcombers worked where they lived – in the slum houses and courtyards surrounding the spinning mills. Often whole families lived in just one room. This was usually the room where the men worked all day at woolcombing. The women and children were working in the local mill, using machinery to spin thread from the wool the men had hand-combed.

The process of woolcombing

The combers worked with raw wool – the oily fleeces straight from the sheep shearers. Their job was to comb the wool so that only the long, straight fibres were left to be spun into thread at the mill. First the combers stoked charcoal stoves until they were hot enough to heat up the metal combs. These were heavy and T-shaped with up to 120 long steel teeth. When the combs were hot enough, the combers fastened one comb to a wooden post and threw a large handful of oily wool onto the hot teeth. Then the combers pulled another hot comb through the wool, unravelling the fibres and laying them straight.

Worsted

To make worsted the raw wool is first combed to separate out the long fibres from the short. The long fibres are then spun to make a strong, supple thread which, when woven, makes a light, smooth fabric.

Woollen cloth

To make woollen cloth the wool is first **carded** so that all the fibres run in the same direction. All the fibres, long and short, are spun into thread which, when woven, makes a dense, solid fabric.

Only one room

This went on until all the fleeces had been combed. The air in the room would be thick with fumes from the charcoal stoves and the stench of oily wool. In the evening the stoves were dampened down and work stopped. The women and children returned from the mill and the room was needed for cooking, eating and sleeping.

Fighting for a fair wage

By the 1820s the woolcombers were becoming discontented. The mill owners were making large profits from worsted manufacturing and the combers felt their wages should be increased. They formed a union, but the mill owners refused to take any notice of it. In 1825 the woolcombers went on strike. It got them nowhere. The owners steadily reduced their wages until, by 1837, woolcombers were earning half the wage of 1825.

Machinery – the final threat

The woolcombers were to face a far bigger threat than harsh mill owners. For some years Samuel Lister had been trying to develop a machine that would comb wool. In 1843 he produced the first sample of machine-combed wool. His machine cost £200 to make   and sold for £1200. Mill owners snapped them up and by the 1850s Samuel Lister was a very rich man. But thousands of woolcombers were thrown out of work. Some re-trained to work on the new machines; many more tried to find other work. But such large-scale unemployment made their situation desperate. Thousands faced starvation.

In 1848, £2000 was allocated by Bradford Council from the city rates to help those woolcombers who wanted to emigrate.

By 1858 no hand-woolcombers were working anywhere in the worsted industry.

Source B

An advertisement written by the Woolcombers' Aid Association in 1848.

Wanted: Situations as Passenger or Goods Porters for 100 Strong, Active, Honest and Industrious Woolcombers from 22 to 40 years of age, varying in height from 5ft 6in to 6ft.

Source C

Part of the report of the Bradford Sanatory Committee on living conditions in Bradford, 1845. Woolcombers lived in the places described here.

Pinfold Street: The back part of the street has filthy yards and cellars in which the inmates are crowded together. The fumes of charcoal breed diseases. Children died of fever here in the last few weeks and women are suffering from various illnesses.

Back Adelaide Street: Very damp – no ventilation – privy [toilet] ten feet three inches from the door – three persons work and sleep in this dirty and confined cellar, five feet three inches below the surface.

Mary Gate: Upper apartment contains three charcoal stoves at which six persons work – there are two beds in the same room in which four persons sleep – bad smell – very hot.

Nelson Court: There are a number of cellars in it utterly unfit for human dwellings. No drainage whatever. The visitors [people writing the report] cannot find words to express their horror of the filth, stench and misery, and were unable to bear the overpowering stench which comes from a common sewer.

Samuel Lister (1815–1906)

Samuel Lister was born in Bradford, West Yorkshire. As a young man, he worked for a firm of Liverpool merchants. Then in 1837 his father built a worsted mill in Bradford and put his two sons, Samuel and John, in charge.

Samuel began inventing. He invented a swivel shuttle and, amongst 150 other things, a loom for weaving velvet. One of his most important inventions was a woolcombing machine. This made him a fortune and brought prosperity to Bradford. He then nearly bankrupted himself developing a machine to spin waste silk. Eventually it was successful, and Samuel made his second fortune.

A grand funeral

On 6 January 1877 the city of Bradford came to a halt. No smoke belched from the hundreds of factory chimneys; flags flew at half-mast; 100,000 people lined the streets and all police leave was stopped. Four horses with black plumes on their heads pulled a **hearse** from Halifax, through Bradford to Saltaire. Seventy carriages followed, carrying the mourners. These were family mourners and anyone of any importance in the industrial north: mill owners and magistrates, MPs and clergymen, peers and chief constables. This was the funeral procession of Titus Salt, one of the most respected mill owners in Yorkshire.

Bradford in the 1830s

In 1834, when he was thirty-one years old, Titus Salt set up his first worsted mill and started to make his fortune. What was Bradford like in the 1830s? It was in the middle of a tremendous upheaval. In 1800 it was a collection of small weaving villages. By 1850 it had 129 factories and a population of over 100,000. Cheap houses were hastily built; roads and sewers couldn't cope. There was terrible overcrowding, dirt and disease in the poorer areas, with clouds of pollution hanging over the whole town.

Making a fortune

By the mid-1840s Titus Salt had made a fortune. This was partly because of **mechanisation**. One by one the processes which converted wool into worsted cloth were taken over by machines. Salt's mills were equipped with spinning machines, then weaving machines and, finally, with combing machines. All this meant that worsted could be produced cheaply – and that it sold well and quickly.

The mystery ingredient

In 1836 Titus Salt made a business trip to Liverpool. There he saw some 300 bales of something called 'Peruvian wool' which no one wanted.

Source A

Titus Salt (1803–76) did not like publicity. This is a rare photograph of him.

Source B

From *Titus Salt and Saltaire* written by John Styles in 1990:

The two waterways that ran through the town – Bradford Beck and the Bradford Canal – were open sewers. In the 1840s the canal was known as 'River Stink'. Smoke poured from factory chimneys, irritating throat and lungs and soiling clothes and buildings.

Average expectation of life in the town in the 1840s was barely twenty years, the lowest in Yorkshire. The rate of infant mortality was the fifth highest in the country.

Popular discontent was shown at meetings and rallies, demonstrations and riots. Bradford was a town where tens of thousands of people took to the streets to demand limits on hours of work in factories, official help for unemployed hand-loom weavers and woolcombers, and the repeal of the hated New Poor Law.

These dresses, the height of fashion in 1862, were made from alpaca. Queen Victoria had several dresses made from alpaca which was specially spun and woven for her in Titus Salt's mills.

Alpaca

Titus took some of this 'wool' home to show his father, who told him not to buy it under any circumstances. Titus bought the whole consignment. With trusted assistants he worked for eighteen months perfecting a way of spinning it into thread. The 'Peruvian wool' was alpaca from Peruvian goats and was to make Titus Salt extremely rich. Titus and his team perfected a way of weaving alpaca with cotton and silk to make a light, slightly shiny cloth which could easily be made up into fashionable women's clothes.

Cornering the market

Titus Salt did not want anyone copying this worsted. It wasn't always easy to get regular supplies from South America. So Salt and two other trusted manufacturers bought up all the supplies of alpaca as soon as they arrived in England. This made sure Salt could keep making this expensive cloth, which rich people would always be able to afford.

A good master

Titus Salt paid good wages and did not lay his workers off when times were bad. This was because his luxury cloth made huge profits. People wanted to work for him, and his workforce was hardworking and loyal. But he was to do more for his workers than this. He moved them out of filthy, polluted Bradford into the purpose-built village of Saltaire.

Source D

From *Salt and Silver* written in 1997 by Jim Greenhalf.

In 1834, when Salt set up in business, alpaca imports amounted to a mere 5,700 lbs. Six years later that had grown to an avalanche: 1,325,000 lbs, most of it arriving in the West Riding [of Yorkshire] by canal barge and cart. For about a quarter of a century from 1840, bright alpaca mixed fabrics took the world by storm.

The Factory Act 1833

This Act applied to textile factories:

- No child under 9 years old could work

- Children aged 9–12 could work for no more than 8 hours a day

- Young people aged 13–18 could work for no more than 12 hours a day

- Working children had to have 2 hours schooling a day

- Four factory inspectors, with sub-inspectors, were appointed to see factory owners obeyed the law.

Children were allowed to work in shifts. This meant that mill owners kept their factories open for the same number of hours and adults had to work for as long, or longer, than before.

Salt's Mill

The mill was the first building to be put up at Saltaire. It was enormous – larger than any mill in Bradford – and had, under one roof, absolutely everything needed to turn wool, cotton, silk and alpaca into a beautiful, glowing and expensive cloth. It was officially opened on 20 September 1853, which was Titus Salt's fiftieth birthday. He held a huge party for 3500 mill workers in the new combing shed. But these mill workers had to travel the three miles from Bradford each day to work in the Saltaire mill and so Titus Salt began to build a village for them on the other side of the railway line from the mill.

Source A

Salt's Mill, the first building in Saltaire. This etching was made in 1885.

Houses

Salt believed that good housing produced good workers. His houses were well built; every one had a yard and an outside lavatory which was emptied regularly. They were carefully graded, according to the occupation of the tenant, and the rent varied according to the size of the house. Workmen's houses had a living room, kitchen and, upstairs, two bedrooms. The houses of overlookers (supervisors) had a **scullery**, kitchen, living room, three bedrooms and a front garden. Managers, designers and wool buyers had the best houses. The streets were named after members of Salt's family, like Albert Road, Ada Street and George Street. By 1871 Titus Salt had built 824 houses in which 4–5000 of his workers lived.

Source B

These are modern photographs of houses in Saltaire. The top picture shows workmen's houses in Ada Street. Those in George Street, below, were for overlookers.

Spare time

Saltaire had churches, almshouses for the elderly, a school and a hospital. But Titus Salt also worried about what his workers would do in their spare time. Spare time, to Salt and other mill owners, meant workers might get drunk, idle or violent.

Source C

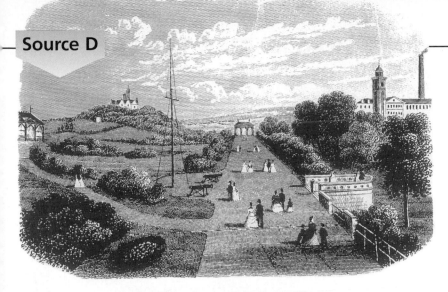

Roberts Park, Saltaire, in 1874. The park covered 14 acres of landscaped ground close to the mill and the church. All sorts of activities were available: swimming, archery, boating, bowls and cricket. There were strict rules: gambling, swearing, stone throwing and drunkenness were forbidden. Dogs were not allowed in the park, neither were children under eight except with an adult.

The Public Health Act 1848

This Act set up a Central Board of Health in London, which was run by three commissioners: Edwin Chadwick, Dr Southwood-Smith and Lord Shaftesbury. This central board had to supervise the setting up of local boards of health in towns and cities throughout Britain.

Local boards were given powers to:

- build sewerage systems
- pipe water to houses
- clean and light streets
- apply building regulations
- appoint a Medical Officer for Health
- raise money from local ratepayers to pay for the improvements.

But the Act only came into force if the death rate in a town was higher than the national average or if 10% of the ratepayers asked for it to apply to their town.

They would also have time to get hold of **Chartist** and **socialist** ideas, and – possibly worst of all – young people would have time for sex. Titus Salt was determined to give his workers suitable ways of spending their leisure time.

He refused to allow any pubs in Saltaire. Instead he gave money to support all sorts of different societies: a cricket club, a fishing club and a gardening society. But more important than the clubs was the Institute. This building held a concert hall, lecture theatre, library, school of art and classrooms. There was also a reading room, chess and draughts room, smoking room, billiards room and gym. It was here that Titus Salt expected his workers to spend most of their spare time. And it was a success. Membership was cheap and the Institute quickly had over a thousand members.

A gentle prison?

Titus Salt was both an employer and a landlord, so he had enormous power over his employees. Workers who were dismissed had to leave the village, so they lost their house and friends as well as their job. Strikes just didn't happen in Saltaire and even trade disputes were rare. It is important to remember that people who went to work for Salt knew what Saltaire was like and knew the sort of standards of behaviour that were expected of them. Many Bradford mill workers sneered and jeered at Salt's workers for being so obedient. However, there were always plenty of people wanting work in Salt's Mill, so perhaps Saltaire gave mill workers were prepared to obey the rules the chance to live in better surroundings.

Early in 1783 a wealthy young man was touring Lancashire on horseback. He seemed particularly interested in rivers and whether they were running swiftly or slowly. What was he doing? He was neither having a holiday nor planning a crime. He was looking for somewhere to build a factory.

Who was Samuel Greg?

Samuel Greg was a very successful textile merchant based in Manchester. The 1780s were exciting times for men like Samuel with money to spend. There were fortunes to be made by people with vision who were willing to take a risk. This was because inventors like James Hargreaves, Richard Arkwright and Samuel Crompton had developed machinery that spun raw cotton quickly and efficiently into thread. Was it worth investing in this new machinery? Samuel thought it was, and decided to take the risk and build a cotton-spinning mill.

Finding a site

Samuel Greg eventually found what he was looking for: a source of power in a valley where it would be possible to build a spinning mill. Ten miles south of Manchester, close to the village of Styal, the river Bollin cut through a sandstone valley. This river, so Samuel believed, was fast-running enough to be able to turn a water wheel and power the spinning mill he was going to build. He checked his figures, and then, in 1784, rented the land and the rights over the water from the Earl of Stamford and Warrington who owned them. Samuel had taken the first steps to becoming a cotton mill owner and the head of a vast business empire.

Source A

Samuel Greg as a young man.

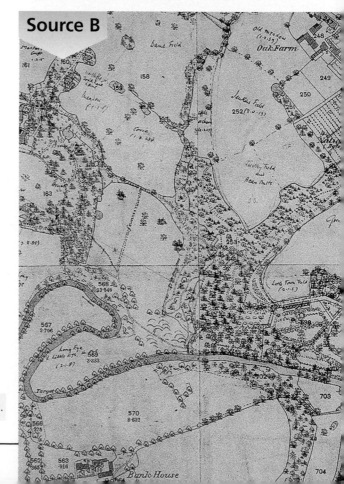

Source B

An eighteenth-century map of the area around Styal.

Finding workers

Samuel Greg had nearly everything he needed for a successful operation: money to build a mill and power to drive the new machinery. But he needed something else: people to work the new machinery. Styal was a small, isolated village. Many people living there worked on the land. Some did a little spinning at home and finished mohair buttons for Macclesfield manufacturers. None of them would ever have worked in a factory and few of them would even have seen one. This doesn't seem to have bothered Samuel Greg. He spent £16,000 building and equipping Quarry Bank Mill and after six years 183 adults and children were working there.

Where had Samuel Greg found his workers? Some were local people. Some came from his works at Eyam in Derbyshire and he may have poached some from other mill owners. However, until the 1840s more than half of his workers were children who came from local workhouses. Greg built a large Apprentice House close to the mill for them, and cottages in Styal village for his adult workers.

A successful enterprise?

Samuel Greg was an **entrepreneur**. He had the money and vision, and was willing to take risks. But he did not have the technical knowledge needed to develop cotton spinning in ways that would bring him most profit. He went into partnership, first with John Massey and then with Peter Ewart. Together they extended the mill buildings to house more machinery, improved the water courses and put in a second water wheel. By the end of the century Samuel Greg was a prosperous mill owner. His gamble had paid off.

Source C

A modern photograph of the front of Quarry Bank Mill, showing the old mill built by Samuel Greg (1784–96) and part of the new mill.

Why build a mill at Styal?

- Cash was available.
- Power was available from the River Bollin.
- New machinery had been invented.
- Wages for mill workers were low.
- 1783: the ending of the American War of Independence opened up new markets for cotton goods.
- 1780s: mill owners no longer had to pay for a licence to use the new inventions.

Using the River Bollin

In 1784, a head-race (channel to take water to the mill) was dug to bring water from the river to power the water wheel. By 1801, Quarry Bank Mill needed more water power. Engineers built a weir across the River Bollin to make a mill pond so that there was always water available to power the water wheel in the mill. In 1820, more water was needed to power a great iron wheel. The mill pond was made bigger and the start of the head-race was improved.

2.11 ESTHER PRICE: A RUNAWAY APPRENTICE

Many jobs in cotton mills could be done by children, such as cleaning under moving machinery or piecing together snapped threads. Children were paid less than adults and were easier to train and discipline. At the time of the first cotton mills, parish authorities were having to deal with large numbers of pauper children. Hundreds of these children were sent to work in cotton mills. Quarry Bank Mill got its children first from the workhouse at Newcastle-under-Lyme and then from the Liverpool workhouse. Around 100 children were sent from Liverpool to Quarry Bank Mill in the 1820s and 1830s. Esther Price was one of these children.

Source A

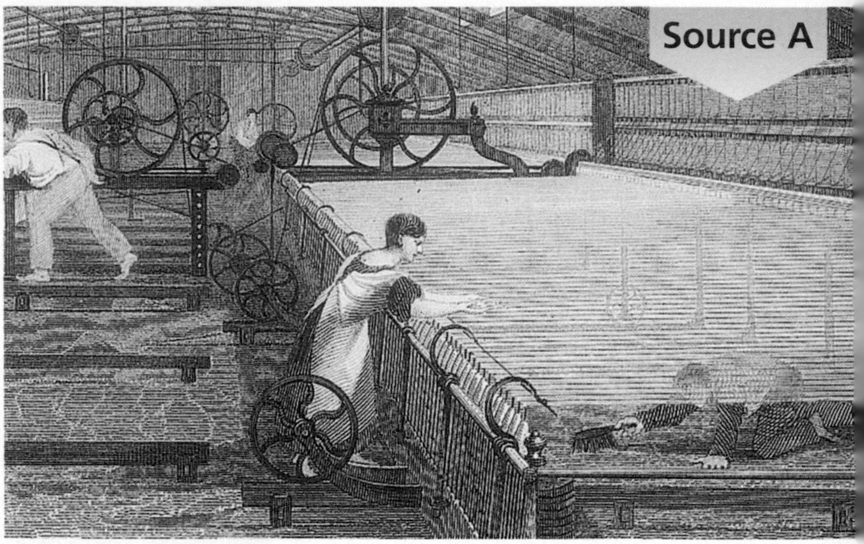

A girl scavenging under a spinning mule. Mules like this were operating in Quarry Bank Mill when Esther Price was there.

From workhouse to Apprentice House

Esther was born in Liverpool on 8 March 1820. She had two brothers, Richard and John, and two sisters, Margaret and Martha. We don't know why, or when, Esther was sent to the workhouse. We don't know whether she went alone or with her whole family. We do know that on 3 May 1831, when Esther was eleven years old, she was at Quarry Bank Mill being examined by the mill's doctor. Samuel Greg would not take weak or sick children. At first, Esther was said to be 'delicate'. The mill's doctor thought she was nine years old, not eleven. However, she must have got stronger because, at the end of 1833, she was legally **apprenticed** to Samuel Greg. Again, there was a muddle about her age. The **indenture** said she was twelve when she was really thirteen years old.

Esther Price's baptismal certificate. This was given to her parents when they took her to church to be baptised.

Source B

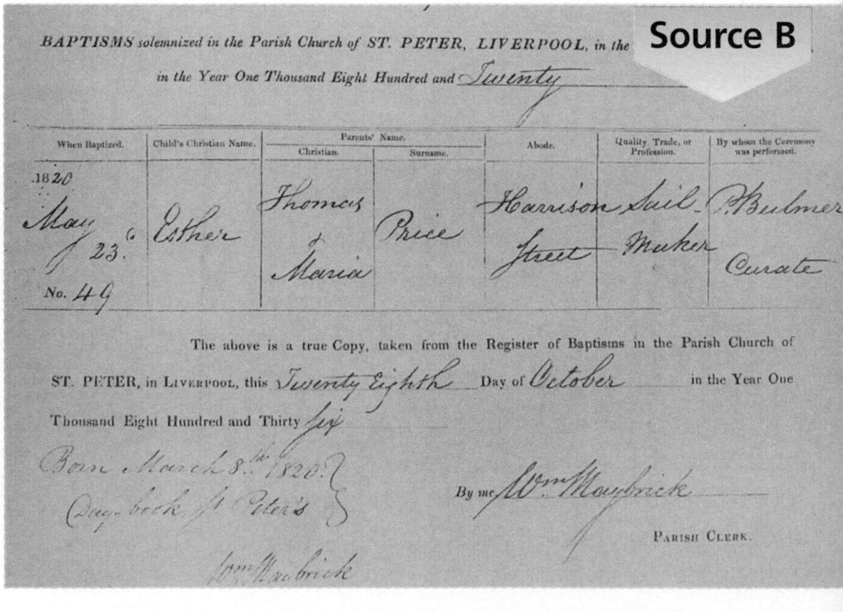

BAPTISMS solemnized in the Parish Church of ST. PETER, LIVERPOOL, in the

in the Year One Thousand Eight Hundred and Twenty

When Baptized.	Child's Christian Name.	Parents' Name. Christian.	Parents' Name. Surname.	Abode.	Quality, Trade, or Profession.	By whom the Ceremony was performed.
1820 May 23. No. 49	Esther	Thomas & Maria	Price	Harrison Street	Sail Maker	P. Bulmer Curate

The above is a true Copy, taken from the Register of Baptisms in the Parish Church of ST. PETER, in LIVERPOOL, this Twenty Eighth Day of October in the Year One Thousand Eight Hundred and Thirty Six

Born March 8th 1820. Day-book St Peter's

By me Wm Maybrick

PARISH CLERK.

Wm Maybrick

A troublesome girl

In August 1835 Mr and Mrs Timperley took over the running of the Apprentice House. Very soon the place was in uproar. In November Esther and another girl assaulted an apprentice so badly that they were sent to the local magistrates' court. Two other girls were given a week's solitary confinement in the Apprentice House for disorderly behaviour.

A modern photograph of the Apprentice House at Quarry Bank Mill. Esther Price lived here 1833–8.

Running away

In August 1836 Esther ran away with her friend Lucy Garner. Lucy went back after five days but Esther stayed away for ten. A pamphlet written at the time says that Esther had gone to Liverpool to see her father while there was no work at the mill. She had asked permission but had been refused. So she took off after work on Saturday and returned at breakfast time on the Wednesday. The mill stopped working on the Monday and Tuesday. Other girls were given permission to visit their parents for quite long periods, but Esther was not.

Punishment

Both girls were put in solitary confinement, Lucy for three days and Esther for a week. Esther was kept in a room in the Apprentice House. The windows were boarded up so that she could neither talk to the others nor escape. She had to sleep on the floor. Every morning and evening she was given milk, bread and porridge to eat. After four days, Mrs Timperley died unexpectedly. Esther, afraid of being left alone with a dead body in the house, begged to be released. She was let out two days early.

Happy endings?

In January 1837 Esther met her sister in the Horseshoe pub. She gave Esther her baptismal certificate. Esther used her baptismal certificate to prove her age and so end her apprenticeship. When her apprenticeship ended, Esther stayed on at the mill for the rest of her working life. Esther's problems were used by supporters of the Ten Hours' Movement, which campaigned for a reduction in the working hours of women and children.

Working conditions

In 1833, a Parliamentary Committee looked at working conditions. William Greg gave evidence about his father's mill at Styal. He said that the apprentices worked a twelve-hour day from Monday to Friday and nine hours on Saturday. After work, the apprentices had to go to school for two hours. He said that they had milk and porridge for breakfast, potatoes and bacon for dinner and meat every Sunday. They always had about 100 apprentices at Styal and when they grew up they usually married amongst themselves and stayed on as adult workers.

The Industrial Revolution brought an increased demand for coal which could not be met simply by extracting coal close to the surface. Instead miners had to sink shafts deep into the ground to tap coal reserves which had formed there. This presented a number of dangers to miners. They ran the risk of injury if their tunnels collapsed and also of drowning if their workings ran into underground springs – or even lakes!

The biggest problem, however, was that of ventilation. Miners needed fresh air to breathe down the pit. They also needed ventilation, which would take away the methane gas given off by the coal and replace it with fresh air. If the gas was not removed then there was a danger that it would be ignited by the miners' candles (it is dark underground!) and an explosion would occur. Unfortunately this is what happened on numerous occasions throughout the eighteenth and nineteenth centuries.

Coursing the air

Various methods were used to get fresh air into the mines. The most common was 'coursing the air'. A second shaft was dug and a large fire placed at the bottom of that shaft. Air heated by the fire rose and 'pulled' fresh air down the first shaft. Partitions were built underground to ensure that the air reached all parts of the mine. If trucks needed to be pushed through the partitions, a child called a trapper would open a door allowing the truck to pass through and close the door after

The importance of coal

Coal was used:
- to heat homes
- to drive factory machinery and steam-powered trains
- to smelt iron
- to make coal gas for heating and lighting
- to make dyes
- to make paint, ink, fertilisers and many other products.

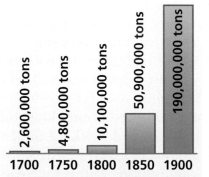

2,600,000 tons	4,800,000 tons	10,100,000 tons	50,900,000 tons	190,000,000 tons
1700	1750	1800	1850	1900

Coal production in Britain 1700–1900.

Source A

An extract from a report on the employment of children in mines in 1842:

They are called trappers. They sit in a little hole and open and shut the doors. They are in the pit the whole time it is worked, frequently about twelve hours a day. They sit in the dark, often with a damp floor. Their ages range from five to ten years.

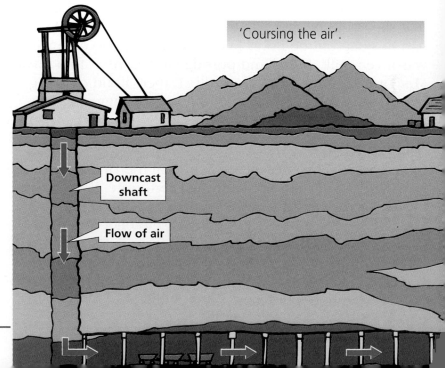

'Coursing the air'.

Downcast shaft

Flow of air

George Stephenson (1781–1848)

Stephenson was the son of a Newcastle colliery engineer. He worked in local pits and is credited with having invented the first miners' safety lamp (though others say Davy was first). He supervised the building of the Stockton-Darlington Railway and his railway engine, *The Rocket*, was used on the Liverpool to Manchester Railway. Stephenson has been called the 'father of the railways'.

To detect the presence of gas, miners often took canaries with them into mines. Canaries have very small lungs and are easily affected by poisonous gas. The miners knew that if the canary stopped singing and fell from its perch, it was time to get out!

The safety lamp

In 1815 Sir Humphrey Davy invented a lamp with **gauze** round it to let out light, but prevent gas from reaching the flame. A similar lamp was invented in the north-east by George Stephenson. These lamps were a great help to miners, but they did not produce very bright light. Some miners actually took the gauze off so that they could see better. Once they had the 'safety lamp', some unscrupulous mine owners sent their employees into areas of the pit which they knew were dangerous, and so accidents did not necessarily decrease.

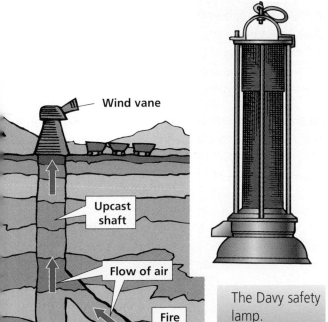

The Davy safety lamp.

Wind vane

Upcast shaft

Flow of air

Fire

Source B

Lord Londonderry, the owner of a mine near Sunderland, speaking in a debate in the House of Lords in 1842:

The Inspectors collect their evidence from artful boys and ignorant young girls. They do this by asking questions which in many cases seemed to suggest the answer. The trapper's work is neither cheerless, nor dull; nor is he kept in loneliness and darkness. There is rarely more than five minutes that passes without some person passing through his door and having a word. The trapper is generally cheerful and contented and to be found, like other children of his age, occupied with some childish amusement – such as cutting sticks.

Source C

An extract from a book written in 1912 in which a retired miner remembers his first day in a pit:

A few hundred yards brought us to a large trap door. This was to be my abiding place for the next twelve or thirteen hours. My father set to work to make a trapper's hole in which I might safely and comfortably sit. He put a nail in the door, to which he fastened my door string, attaching the other end of it to a nail in a prop where I sat, so that I could pull the door open when the horse and wagons were coming through. Several men passing through my door at various times spoke kindly to the new trapper and told me to take care and keep in my hole. One man who came through looked very different from the other men, for his face and hands were clean, his jacket was buttoned and his shirt looked very white. He was a big man and carried a stick. He looked very sternly at me and holding his stick up in a threatening way he said 'If you go to sleep and don't keep that door shut, you'll get it.'

Disaster in the pit

As the demand for coal grew during the Industrial Revolution, thousands of small 'pit villages' sprang up in the main coalfields of Britain. One area where this was particularly true was north-east England. In the Northumberland and Durham coalfields there were hundreds of pits and many of them were surrounded by small villages, which existed simply because the pit was there.

In such villages the whole population depended upon the pit. Those who were not working there had jobs which supplied miners and their families with their food and clothing or helped run the service industries that kept a village alive. Everyone had friends or relatives that worked in the pit and everyone lived in fear that one of the regular disasters that occurred in the mining industry would happen to their pit.

On 25 May 1812 the people of Felling felt the ground shake under their feet. They knew their worst fears were about to come true.

Source D

An extract from the list of those killed at Felling Colliery, 25 May 1812:

Name	Job	Age
Thomas Craggs	Hewer	36
Thomas Craggs	Trapper	9
John Greener	Hewer	21
Edward Richardson	Hewer	39
Robert Dobson	Trapper	13
William Dixon	Hewer	35
George Robson	Putter	15
Andrew Allan	Trapper	11
John Thompson	Hewer	36
John Pearson	Hewer	64
Thomas Bears	Hewer	48
Charles Wilson	Hewer	48
Joseph Gordon	Trapper	10
Robert Gordon	Hewer	40
Thomas Gordon	Trapper	8

Explosion at Felling pit!

The pit at Felling began work in May 1811. The best methods of ventilation known at the time were used, but in spite of this the pit exploded on 25 May 1812.

The deep places where the explosions took place restricted the force so that the full noise was not heard on the surface. For half a mile the trembling of the ground was the first sign of the explosion and then for four miles the noise of hollow rumblings in the air was heard. Immense quantities of coal, pieces of wood and dust drove high in the air and some bodies of injured men were thrown up the shaft.

The scene was dreadful, in all directions roads and paths were covered with coal dust and bits of machinery and the area was enveloped in darkness. The explosion had wrecked all the machinery and it was not until fresh machinery could be brought that steps could be taken to see what had happened. When this was done only 32 out of the 120 men and boys employed in the mine were rescued alive. Three of these died afterwards, suffering from burns and injuries.

After the blast some fearless men descended into the pit to see what had happened, but after a few attempts they had to return to the surface without being able to tell those waiting what had happened to their menfolk and children. The pit owners decided to put the fire out by sealing the pit and depriving it of oxygen.

The pit was not re-opened until 7 July 1812, when a great cloud of smoke came out of the shaft. Despite the time the pit had been closed, a great crowd of people assembled at the pit head hoping that their relatives might still be alive. When men descended into the pit they saw a horrific sight. Masses of rock had been hurled in every direction, wagons shattered and twisted, bodies of men, so mutilated that they could not be recognised.

From a report of the Felling Pit Disaster written shortly after the explosion.

Source E

Deaths in pits in the north-east 1793–1813.

This list was produced in the nineteenth century and the compiler wrote: 'Note this list is necessarily incomplete because of the lack of records.'

Date		Pit	Deaths
27 Dec	1793	Sheriff Hall, Gateshead	14
9 June	1794	Picton	30
11 June	1794	Harraton, Chester-le-Street	28
24 April	1795	Benwell, Newcastle	11
11 Oct	1799	Lumley	39
25 Sept	1803	Wallsend	13
21 Oct	1805	Hepburn, Newcastle	35
29 Nov	1805	Oxclose	38
28 March	1806	Killingworth	10
14 Sept	1809	Killingworth	12
25 May	1812	Felling	92
10 Oct	1812	Herrington	24
28 Sept	1813	Fatfield	32
24 Dec	1813	Felling	22

Source F

A trapper at work underground. This picture was produced in a government report on the employment of children in 1842.

Jobs done in the mine

Trapper: A child who opened and closed ventilation doors underground.

Hewer: A miner who cut the coal underground using a pick axe.

Putter: A miner (usually a young man) who pushed the coal tubs between the coal face and the shaft bottom.

Source G

These words were found scratched onto a water bottle belonging to Michael Smith. He was one of 164 miners who died after being trapped underground in an explosion at Seaham Colliery in County Durham in 1880.

Dear Margaret

There were forty of us all together at 7 a.m. Some were singing hymns, but my thoughts were on my little Michael, that he and I would meet in heaven at some time. Oh dear wife, God save you and the children and pray for me. Dear wife farewell, my last thoughts are about you and the children. Be sure and learn the children to pray for me. Oh what an awful position we are in.

Children in the mines

Today there would be serious trouble if an employer sent a young child to work in a dangerous environment like a mine. Indeed it would be illegal for a child of eight to be employed doing any job.

But this was not the case in the early eighteenth century. Children as young as seven or eight would work in the dark depths of the mine, opening and closing trap doors. As they became older and stronger, the children would be put to work carrying loads from the coal face to tubs at the bottom of the shaft.

There were many complaints about children working in mines at the time and a government report in 1842 talked of how 'no sooner are the children strong enough, then they become underground machines, without the slightest education'.

But for children of miners the idea of working underground was something they were used to. They were brought up expecting to earn their keep as soon as they were old enough. Their families needed the money that they would earn and some children were keen to start work as early as possible.

Roads

Most roads in the eighteenth century were muddy tracks linking village to village and villages to market towns. Pack horses and large wagons carried goods; business men travelled by horseback. Most other people walked. But change was on the way.

Turnpike Trusts

Turnpike Trusts were groups of people who got together to keep a stretch of road in good repair. They put gates and toll-houses at each end and charged travellers for using the road. Turnpikes employed specialist road builders, including Thomas Telford (1757–1834) and John McAdam (1756–1836). The roads they built meant that long distance travellers could use wheeled coaches. By about 1800 all of the larger towns in Britain were connected by turnpike roads.

Stagecoaches and mail coaches

Stagecoaches made their journeys in regular stages; hence the name. While stable-lads changed the horses, passengers would have a quick meal at the inn before setting off again. In 1784 the Post Office started running mail coaches and by 1792 there were 150 specially built coaches on the road. They carried passengers as well, but they had a rough ride until 1805 when Obadiah Elliott invented metal coach springs! Goods carriers copied the stagecoaches by running a timetabled service, and they, like the mail coach operators, allowed passengers to sit amongst the parcels.

Source A

This painting from 1839 shows a stagecoach passing through a turnpike at night.

Source B

William Cobbett, writing in 1818, describes the scene at a coaching inn:

The beautiful horses, impatient to be off. The inside of the coach full and the outside covered with men, women and children, boxes, bags and bundles. The coachman taking his reins in one hand and the whip in the other gives a signal with his foot and away they go at a speed of seven miles per hour. One of these coaches coming in, after a long journey, is a fascinating sight. The horses are all sweat and foam. Everything is covered with dust and dirt. But it still comes in, as regular as the hands of a clock.

Source C

Turnpiked and unturnpiked roads in 1838.

Turnpiked road = 21,735 miles
Typical journey time = 7 miles per hour

Unturnpiked road = 103,707 miles
Typical journey time = 3 miles per hour

Canals

Road improvements helped people to move around the country, but it was difficult and expensive to transport heavy goods in that way. Rivers and the sea were used to transport goods like coal and iron, but not every merchant worked close to the coast or to a navigable river. Canals were the answer. These were artificial waterways used to join up existing rivers. The very first canal was the Sankey Cut. It opened in 1757 for barges to carry Lancashire coal to Liverpool. Four years later the Duke of Bridgewater paid for a canal to carry coal from his mine at Worsley to Manchester. From then on, canals were paid for by groups of investors.

Canal mania

Canals were expensive to build. The men who invested money in them hoped to be rich. In the 1790s there was a mad rush to invest in canals. Many silly and impractical schemes were dreamed up and a lot of people lost a lot of money. But the good schemes worked. The Leeds to Liverpool canal, for example, was finished in 1816 and was a great success. As well as carrying heavy raw materials, canals were also good at transporting delicate, breakable goods. Josiah Wedgwood, whose company made fine china, invested in canals and used them because they transported his product smoothly.

The most important canals in Britain in about 1830. Canals linked almost all of England to the four major ports of London, Bristol, Liverpool and Hull.

Source E

Forth and Clyde Canal
Leeds and Liverpool Canal
Leeds
Liverpool
Hull
Bridgewater Canal
Manchester
Coventry Canal
Grand Trunk or Trent and Mersey Canal
Birmingham
Staffs and Worcs Canal
Oxford Canal
Grand Union Canal
Monmouth Canal
Bristol
London
Kennet and Avon Canal

Canals
Navigable rivers

0 — 50 miles
0 — 80 km

James Brindley (1716–72)

Born near Buxton in Derbyshire, James soon moved with his family to Leek. Although he never learned to read and write, in 1742 James Brindley set up as a millwright in Leek. He began work on many engineering projects, including a windmill for grinding flints, and a steam powered engine. In 1759 the Duke of Bridgewater employed him to build a canal 67.5km long to take coal from his estate, near Wigan, to Manchester and then on to the River Mersey. Altogether Brindley surveyed and supervised the building of hundreds of miles of canals. He was the first canal builder to use tunnels and aqueducts instead of locks.

Railways

The very first railways were on the coalfields, where horses pulled coal wagons along wooden rails. Coal mines had steam engines, too, but these were used to pump water out of the mine workings. Sometimes fixed engines were used to winch wagons along the rails.

The first steam train

It was Richard Trevithick, a Cornish mining engineer, who hit upon the idea of combining a fixed iron rail with a moving steam engine. In 1804 his steam engine pulled five wagons, a coach and seventy passengers from the Pen-y-Daren **ironworks** in South Wales to the Glamorganshire canal. However, Richard Trevithick did not have the money to develop his steam engine, nor could he find wealthy people to back him. He died, a poor man, in 1833. Others, however, realised the importance of what he had done. They took his brilliant idea and carried it further than even he could have dreamed.

A railway network

In 1825 a steam engine called *Locomotion* pulled a train from Stockton to Darlington. Five years later the Prime Minister, the Duke of Wellington, opened a railway between Liverpool and Manchester. He travelled in the train, pulled by an engine called *The Rocket*. It was a great success, even though, at the opening, William Huskisson, MP for Liverpool, was knocked down by a passing train and later died.

People rushed to put money into railways and many new lines were built. During this 'railway mania' some people lost thousands of pounds putting money into crazy schemes. However, by 1855 more than 8000 miles of track linked all the major cities in Britain and the railways were carrying more goods than the canals.

Arguments against the railway at the time.

- Canal transport would end.
- There would be soot everywhere.
- Turnpike trusts would go bust.
- Fox hunting would be ruined.
- Milking would be affected.
- Women would miscarry.
- Sparks would cause fires.
- There would be railway tracks everywhere.
- Fast travel would send people mad.

The Railway Station painted in 1862 by William Powell Frith.

Britain's railway network in 1852.

Richard Trevithick (1771–1833)

Richard Trevithick was born in Cornwall. His father was a mine manager and Richard learned a lot about the practical problems of mining and about engines and pumps. In 1797, he was appointed engineer at the Ding Dong mine near Penzance where he built high-pressure steam engines.

He was a brilliant engineer and inventor. It was Richard Trevithick who realised that his light, powerful steam engine could be put on a cart and run along fixed rails. In 1804, his was the first steam engine to run on rails and pull a train.

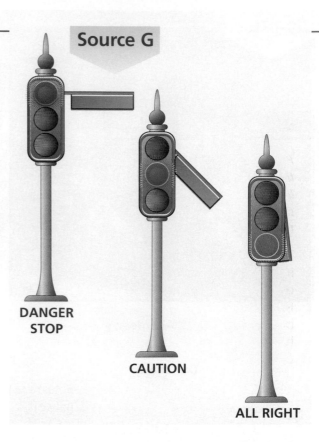

Source G

DANGER
STOP

CAUTION

ALL RIGHT

The standard signalling rules which Neele helped to develop.

George Neele, superintendent of the London and Northwestern Railway

George Neele worked in railways all his life. In 1846, aged 21, he was working for the Eastern Counties Railway at Ely as a clerk. Promotion came quickly. By 1862 he was superintendent of the London and Northwestern Railway, the largest of all the railway companies operating in Great Britain. He stayed there as superintendent until he retired in 1895. At his funeral in 1921, six London and Northwestern railway guards carried his coffin.

In 1904 George wrote a book called *Railway Reminiscences* in which he put down what he could remember of his working life. These extracts are taken from his book; some are in his own words (in *italics*) and some have been shortened.

Where's that train?

The sight of the steam by day and the headlight at night, or of the whistle of the approaching engine, formed the only means of information for the station master or porter who had to be on the look-out on the platform.

In the 1840s the telegraph was used on certain sections of some lines; the telephone was in fairly general use in the 1880s, but it was not until around 1910 that full traffic control systems were used on all main lines.

Signals

George Neele played an important part in developing a set of standard signals and signalling rules which were eventually accepted by all the British railway companies (see Source G).

Accident at Abergele, 1868!

George was on holiday at Lowestoft when the Irish mail train crashed outside Abergele in North Wales. He broke off his holiday to help with the investigation. An account of the accident was written in a letter to *The Times* newspaper by the Marquis of Hamilton, who was in one of the rear carriages with his wife and family. Here George writes about the letter:

He describes how immediately after the collision he got down from the train and saw the whole of the three front passenger carriages, the vans and the engines, enveloped in sheets of flame, and dense smoke rising 20ft high and spreading in every direction. The wreck was the work of an instant; not a movement of any sort, no struggle to escape, was apparent from the doomed carriages. Their contents of charred and mutilated remains were discovered an hour afterwards.

The Irish mail train had collided with four runaway wagons of petroleum.

A late nineteenth-century steam train.

Tourist train wrecked at Wigan, 1873!

For some reason the 16th carriage from the front broke away and, turning to the left, took with it the whole of the rest of the train. The first eight vehicles became a total wreck, with a terrible loss of life.

This accident was the first to be investigated by a public inquiry. The chief officials of the London and Northwestern Railway clearly thought the accident had been caused by speed. They believed they had to maintain high speeds because of competition from other lines.

Queen Victoria's train journeys

George Neele travelled with the Queen's train on her journeys to and from Scotland. Altogether he made 112 of these journeys.

1865
At Forfar, just as the Queen's train approached, one of the yardmen of the Scottish Northeastern took across the two main lines a goods wagon hauled by a horse, and had barely cleared the track when the train came up. Mr Esplin, the manager of the line, was in the Royal train, but the narrow escape did not appear to disturb him. All we could gather from him was that the yardman stated he did not know of the Royal train's coming: he had not noticed and went on with his work as usual.

1872
Passing along the platform in the dead of night at Wigan I was surprised to find John Brown (the Queen's servant) and on enquiring whether all was right, heard to my surprise, 'No! The Queen says the carriage is shaking like the devil.' But this certainly was only John Brown's way of putting it.

1884
On arrival at Oxford a note was received from the Queen complaining that gas had been introduced into the lights in her saloon instead of oil, and requesting an alteration. The substitution of oil then was impossible! The glare of the gas in the globes, which unfortunately were plain and not frosted, was the cause of annoyance, and I had the supply reduced as far as possible, to be of service.

The battle of the gauges

The distance between rails on a rail track is called the gauge. George Stephenson laid his rails about 1.5m apart. Isambard Kingdom Brunel laid his rails about 2m apart. Speed trials were held. Engines running on the wider gauge went faster and had fewer accidents than those on the narrower gauge. Even so, Parliament decided to make Stephenson's gauge standard throughout Britain. It was more expensive to widen a track than to narrow it and 1900 miles of Stephenson's gauge track had already been built compared with 274 of Brunel's.

We have seen how the Industrial Revolution affected people in Britain who worked in mines and factories and who had to live in industrial towns. But these were not the only people to be affected. There were changes, too, in the lives of the wealthy and their servants.

LADY CHARLOTTE GUEST

Lady Charlotte Guest was married to John Guest, who ran the Dowlais ironworks near Merthyr Tydfil, Wales. They married in 1833, when she was 21 and he was 48. Between 1833 and 1852 (the year John died) they had ten children. Lady Charlotte took an interest in the Dowlais works. The works made iron that was bought by railway companies and other industries. So Lady Charlotte was more involved in the Industrial Revolution than the wife of a country landowner would have been. But her diary, from which the following extracts come, are as full of parties and politics as they are of industry. Like many well-off women at the time, Lady Charlotte busied herself with working for the poor. She set up schools at Dowlais, both for the children of the workers and for the men.

Source A

Cynfarthfa Ironworks, painted in about 1870. Cynfarthfa was also in Merthyr Tydfil, and was owned by the Crawshay family.

Railways

Lady Charlotte and her husband travelled often. They usually went by coach, but they started to use railways more and more:
Then we caught the railway. We had two seats in the Mail part of the train. Our carriage was lashed onto a machine behind. We sent the servants to ride in that. The 36 miles took an hour and a half. By coach it would have taken us over four hours. It is much smoother and easier than a carriage and the speed is not alarming, because it is so steady.

Lady Charlotte laid the foundation stone for the Taff Vale Railway, on 16 August 1837:
I laid the mortar with a pretty little trowel. When the stone was lowered, the Engineer brought me an equally small hammer to strike it into place. I insisted on using a big wooden mallet, much to the amusement of the workmen.
Rail travel was not always as pleasant as Lady Charlotte's first experience. In July 1838:
I travelled part of the way home on the Great Western Railway. It is new, but rocked the whole way, like a steamship. There are many men already mending the line.

Factories

Interested people would visit factories regularly:

4 November 1833: *We were up early this morning to see Mr Houldsworth's cotton factory, which he kindly showed us over.*

I have never seen anything of the kind before, and was much pleased with the machinery. The process of passing the threads through a gas light, to take off the imperfections, is the prettiest part of the process. We then saw velvet embroidered by machine. We went, after, to Sharpe and Roberts's where there is all sorts of machinery. They were making a steam coach. A movable platform took people from the top storey to the bottom, instead of stairs. This is also a useful machine for loading wagons.

Cholera

Even outlying places, like Dowlais, were not free from the threat of cholera, which struck in 1849:

31 May: *The cholera has broken out with great violence in Cardiff. John has been to a meeting about cleaning the town. Dowlais is to be whitewashed and cleaned as much as possible. The doctor has set up a system of house-to-house visits to check if anyone has the early symptoms.*

9 June: *The cholera is still raging, and has crept gradually to Gellivaelog, just across the river from Dowlais.*

11 June: *A letter from Dr White reports the first case of cholera at Dowlais. His visitors now have much to do on the house-to-house searches. People are so alarmed and frightened that many imagine symptoms that are not there. The doctors will be worn out before the cholera sets in.*

22 June: *The cholera is worse at Dowlais. Thirteen deaths a day. I have sent asking for more medical help.*

31 July: *The children and I are now in the country. The cholera at Dowlais is so bad. Twenty or more dying a day. Eight men constantly employed in coffin-making.*

Lady Charlotte giving prizes at Dowlais school in about 1855.

Source B

The Great Exhibition, 1851

Lady Charlotte went to the Great Exhibition:

Some days before a great deal was said about the dangers: some said the whole building would tumble down, some that the noise of the cannons would shatter the glass. Others feared the masses would riot. But it was, instead, the most dazzling sight I ever saw. Everyone behaved perfectly.

Domestic service

The numbers of people working in factories rose rapidly during the Industrial Revolution. Even so, most women worked in **domestic service**. Most men worked in farming, but the second biggest employer of men was domestic service. Unlike factories and mines, no **commissions** were set up to investigate the working conditions of servants. No laws were passed about the age at which a child could go into service, or their hours, or wages. Servants were a fact of life. They had always been there, absolutely necessary to those who used them, but invisible. Did the Industrial Revolution affect them? It depended on their job and their employer.

HARRIET BROWN

In 1870 Harriet Brown, new in service, wrote to her mother: *I am up at half past five or six each morning and do not go to bed till midnight. I do the fires and just keep on, all day. I feel so tired sometimes I have a good cry. Mrs Graves the cook is very kind. She helped me with my work this morning, or I would never have got through it. I would like to ask you to visit next week, but we have two dinner parties and shall be ever so busy. I can give you plenty of mending, when there is time, but I do not know when that will be.*

Twenty years later Harriet was a married woman sending her daughter Ellen into service. Ellen worked the same hours and cried herself to sleep, too. Those starting at the bottom of the servant ladder always had the hardest time of it.

Source C

Who were servants?

Domestic servants worked in other people's homes, doing the work that kept the house and garden running.

Rich people with huge houses and grounds could have over a hundred servants. Servants lived in their own part of the house or grounds and all had a particular job to do. There were men to open the front door, do the gardening and look after the horses. There were housemaids who dusted, cooks, and scullery maids who washed up. Important servants, such as the butler and the lady's maid, had nothing to do with the boy who cleaned the boots and shoes or the girl who did the washing up!

At the other end of the scale, in poorer households, was the young girl who came in each day from her own home to help. She did everything, from cleaning to looking after the children.

The men who worked at Petworth House in the 1870s. They are (from left to right along each row, top to bottom) the assistant under butler, a footman, the under butler, another footman, the house steward, the lodge keeper, the chef, another lodge keeper, a footman, the steward's room man, the second chef and the final footman

A servant's life was not always dull. Here a servant who left to marry has come back for a visit. Everyone has stopped for a cup of tea and a chat. It is unlikely that the cook, returning from her afternoon out, will approve!

Changes?

In the 1890s more people began to have labour-saving devices in their home, to reduce the work for servants. They also began to give servants more time off. They could have an afternoon at the cinema, or an evening at the **music hall**. Some servants even got a whole day off, so they could use **excursion trains** to have a day at the seaside or in London. More and more servants benefited from the changes brought by the Industrial Revolution. Why? Because by this time there was a shortage of servants. People who had once gone into service, especially women, found there were other jobs they could do which gave them more freedom and better wages; new jobs, created by new inventions. They could work at a **telephone exchange** or as a secretary, although they needed some education for these jobs.

WILLIAM LANCERLY

I began in service as a boot boy, aged sixteen. I had to clean boots and shoes, sharpen knives, fetch and carry, trim the lamp wicks (the house had no gas or electric), lay up and wash up for the servants' meals, clean the windows, mirrors and the silver and help to carry and wait when there were people to dinner. After two years I was made footman. After four years I was given a holiday, because the family would be away from home. I had three whole days. In this time I visited London, and decided to get a job with a family with a Town House there. So I did. My duties there were light, I was even given an evening off from time to time to go to the theatre. But there was no chance of promotion, so I moved on. When I eventually had to appoint servants myself, I found that farmers' children or servants' children were best because they were used to early rising and hard work.

Mrs Layton

In 1931, at 71 years old, Mrs Layton told of her life in service:
When I was ten I went to mind the baby of a person who ran a small shop. I got to work at eight in the morning and left at eight at night except for two nights when I was allowed to leave at seven to go to a night school. I grew fond of the baby, but when my mistress insisted that I leave the school to work the extra hours I refused. When I was thirteen I went into service at Hampstead, where I stayed a year. I had a kind mistress, and plenty of good food. But I had to sleep in the basement kitchen, which swarmed with black beetles at night.

In 1775, Britain's American colonies decided they had had enough of British rule. They drove out the British, wrote a *Declaration of Independence*, and set about working out how thirteen states with different laws and attitudes, not least of all to slavery, could work together as a 'nation'. Newspapers and speeches were full of ideas about '**liberty**' and 'the rights of man'. These ideas spread across the sea to Europe, which spent the rest of the century trying to cope with them.

Liberty and equality?

In many countries the gulf between rich and poor, between those with power and those without, seemed vast, with one law for the rich and another for the poor. When, in 1789, Paris exploded into a **revolution** that swept across France, some people saw it as a good thing. Conditions for many people in France had been appalling. The new government's *Declaration of the Rights of Man* (Source A) sounded perfectly reasonable. However, when the King and nobles who had 'oppressed the poor' were executed by the newly-invented **guillotine**, people abroad began to get nervous. A Revolutionary Government was set up to make sure reforms – including fixing the price of bread, and free education – were carried out all over France. But it soon became more concerned with keeping hold of power. It became more and more extreme, and sent people to the guillotine at an ever-increasing rate. What next? Would this unrest spread?

Source A

The main points of the *Declaration of the Rights of Man*, 26 August 1789:

- **Men are born free, with equal rights.**
- **No one should rule without the support of the people.**
- **All people can have a say in government, themselves or by a representative, who must explain his actions to them.**
- **One person's liberty must not hurt another's.**
- **People can only be arrested if they break the law.**
- **Everyone is innocent until proven guilty.**
- **People can have their own political and religious beliefs.**
- **Police will enforce the law, for the public good, not for their own gain.**
- **People will give money to run the country, according to what they can give. They must be told how it is spent.**

Monarchy (Louis XVI)	Revolutionary Government	Emperor Napoleon	Monarchy restored	Republic
1786	1794	1815	1830 1848	1849

The government of France 1786–1849.

A cartoon drawn in the 1790s showing possible effects of the French Revolution on the other countries of Europe.

Watching France

The rest of Europe watched France uneasily. It seemed that the events there were affecting the rest of Europe. The 1789 Revolution in France sparked off unrest in other countries. This was snuffed out, but left governments worried. When France was settled, Napoleon Bonaparte made himself emperor and began a series of wars trying to take over all of Europe. Later rebellions in France, in 1830 and 1848, often sparked risings in the rest of Europe. Most failed. Some, like Belgium's attempt to break away from Holland in 1830, succeeded.

What about Britain?

Britain avoided a revolution at this time. The government made just enough reforms to keep people happy. Even so, when ordinary people held rallies and mass meetings about the right to vote, the government reacted sharply. If they left things too long, it could get out of hand – just look at France. When hungry agricultural workers marched, setting fire to hayricks, even farms, the government was even more worried. After all, rising bread prices had set the French Revolution going.

The government often reacted harshly. It sent a group of labourers from Tolpuddle to Australia for seven years' hard labour (see pages 24–5). Their 'crime' was not striking, or causing a riot, but joining a trade union. This was not actually illegal, so they were prosecuted for swearing an illegal oath instead. In 1819, magistrates sent armed soldiers to attack a crowd (which included women and children) at a meeting at St Peter's Field, Manchester about political reform. We know a revolution did not break out, but the government feared it was just around the corner.

The Peterloo Massacre

The riots in St Peter's Fields, Manchester, 1819, came to be called 'The Peterloo Massacre'. The large crowd, some 50,000 men, women and children were mainly working class and were unarmed. It was called the Peterloo massacre after the biggest battle within living memory – Waterloo. The area looked like a battle field when the soldiers were done.

3.2 THE AMERICAN REVOLUTION

The thirteen British colonies in America were set up at various times, by different groups of people. They had their own local governments, laws, religions, even money. They squabbled with each other, especially over the boundaries between them. Yet by 1775 Britain had managed to make them so angry that they united to force Britain to give them **independence**. How did Britain so mismanage relations with the American colonies? Partly, it was reacting to a fear that it might lose the colonies to Britain's old enemy, France.

War with France

Britain and France both had colonies in America and in Canada. They both wanted to gain more land – from each other. In 1756 Britain and France went to war in America. The British colonies all sent soldiers to fight the French and when the British won, in 1763, the colonists went home expecting gratitude, even rewards. But Britain was determined to keep a tight grip on the colonies.

British interference

Instead of being grateful, the British passed laws that seemed mistrustful of the colonists. These laws stipulated with whom the colonies could, and could not, trade and doubled the taxes the colonists had to pay on goods from Europe. Britain told its colonies to set up armies or pay to keep a British defence force there. The colonies did neither. So, in 1765, Parliament set up a new tax, the Stamp Tax, to pay for a British defence force. Everything that was bought or sold had to have a stamp, which had to be paid for. The colonists refused to pay. They rioted. The British governors wrote frantic letters home and the Stamp Act was **repealed**.

Growing unity

Britain's laws applied to all the colonies. Each new law gave the colonies a greater sense of unity and shared injustice. As the British taxed more goods, the colonies organised and acted together. They refused to buy British goods. The British were forced to stop the new taxes, all except the one on tea. This started a riot in Boston. British soldiers, in a panic, fired on the crowd and five people were killed. The 'Boston Massacre' set off a stream of political pamphlets against the British.

The thirteen British colonies in 1775.

A painting of the Battle of Princetown, 3 January 1777. The man on the white horse leading the American soldiers on the left of the picture (the British are on the right, in red coats) is General George Washington.

The colonies set up a secret information network, ready to organise the war with the British which now seemed inevitable.

The war

British attempts to collect taxes led to protests. The British closed the port of Boston after the colonists dumped a shipload of British tea in the harbour (an event known as the 'Boston Tea Party'). Other places did the same. The colonists were becoming more openly defiant. The British closed the Virginian governing body to strike against colonial local government, so the Virginians set up their own government and a Congress of the States. The secret network was out in the open. The British army met at Lexington in 1775, to march on Concord, where there was a rebel arms store. The rebels in Lexington sent a message to the people in Concord to be ready. The war began. The rebels published a formal Declaration of Independence from Britain in July 1775. At first everyone thought the rebels would be beaten easily. But the war dragged on for six long years, until September 1781 when the British surrendered at Yorktown. In 1783 the official peace treaty was signed. The rebels had won. They could begin to become Americans.

Becoming American

The colonies had been united in their need to get rid of the British. But once rid of a common enemy, the states began to remember all the things that made them different. The governing body, Congress, could not pull them all into line. One man, Ethan Allen, made it clear that he and his men had fought for independence for Vermont, and that if they did not get it he would *retire to the mountains to wage war on all humanity*. He didn't. Instead he plotted with the British to make Vermont a British colony again, although this failed through lack of support. When Congress eventually drew up a plan for governing the states, it had to have two levels. Some decisions were made for all the states by Congress. But local matters were to be decided by state governments.

George Washington (1732–99)

George Washington led the American armies to victory in the war with the British rebels, 1775–1781. He became the first President of the United States in 1789. When invited to rule as a king, he said: 'It is an idea I view with abhorrence and reprimand with severity'.

Paul Revere – hero of the American Revolution

*Listen my children and you shall hear
Of the midnight ride of Paul Revere,*

began a poem by the poet Henry Longfellow. The poem goes on to tell in great (sometimes inaccurate) detail how Paul Revere, hero of the American Revolution, took the news of the advance of the British army from Boston to Lexington, then Concord.

Who was Paul Revere?

Paul Revere was one of the early organisers of the 'Sons of Liberty' who spoke out against British taxes. He was a silversmith and engraver who also published anti-tax pamphlets. He was one of the riders who took news and messages from colony to colony as they organised themselves. He is said to have taken part in the 'Boston Tea Party' (where some of the Sons of Liberty, disguised as Indians, threw British tea into the harbour). He then took the news to other states. He set up a system of lantern signals to send a warning of the British army's advance.

What happened?

Almost everyone in Boston knew the British army intended to march. On 18 April 1775, they set off. Revere was rowed across the Charles River from Boston to Charlestown. He rode towards Concord. All along the way he woke people and warned them to be ready. A man called William Dawes was sent to do the same job by a different route. By midnight Revere was in Lexington where he met up with Dawes. They set off for Concord, joined by Dr Samuel Prescott, who lived in Concord but had been visiting his girlfriend in Lexington. Prescott is not known to have taken an active part in activities against the British before.

They met a British army patrol. Dawes escaped to Lexington. Revere was captured. His horse was taken from him and he was forced to walk back to Lexington. The final, vital, leg of the ride was made by Prescott, who jumped his horse over a fence and made it to Concord.

Source B

Even after the American Revolution, fighting, mainly at sea, continued between the British and the Americas. This picture, painted in 1815, shows one such clash.

Part of *Paul Revere's Ride*, by Henry Wadsworth Longfellow:

*Listen my children and you shall hear
Of the midnight ride of Paul Revere,
On the eighteenth of April in Seventy-five;
Hardly a man is now alive
Who remembers that famous day and year.*

*It was twelve by the village clock,
When he crossed the bridge into Medford
    town.
He heard the crowing of the cock,
And the barking of the farmer's dog,
And felt the damp of the river fog,
That rises after the sun goes down.*

*It was one by the village clock
When he galloped into Lexington.
He saw the gilded weathercock
Swim in the moonlight as he passed.
And the meetinghouse windows, blank and
    bare,
Gaze at him with a spectral glare
As if they already stood aghast
At the bloody work they would look upon.*

*It was two by the village clock
When he came to the bridge in Concord
    town.
He heard the bleating of the flock,
And the twitter of birds among the trees
And felt the breath of the morning breeze
Blowing over the meadows brown.
And one was safe and asleep in his bed,
Who at the bridge would be first to fall,
Who that day would be lying dead
Pierced by a British musket ball.*

*So through the night rode Paul Revere;
And so through the night went his cry of
    alarm
To every Middlesex village and farm,
A cry of defiance and not of fear,
A voice in the darkness, a knock at the
    door,
And a word that shall echo for evermore!*

Source C

Paul Revere's ride was still being sung about in 1900.

Longfellow (1807–82)

Henry Wadsworth Longfellow was born in Maine and went to Harvard University. He was famous for his poetry on historical themes. As well as *Paul Revere's Ride* he wrote a long poem, *The Song of Hiawatha* about Native American life.

Longfellow translated the works of the poet Dante into English. He also campaigned against slavery, writing a number of anti-slavery poems and songs. When John Brown led a raid to rescue slaves in the southern states, Longfellow remarked that the raid was 'the dawn of a new revolution, quite as much needed as the old one'.

3.3 THE GIFT OF LIBERTY

Source A

The Statue of Liberty is one of the most famous symbols of America today. She stands at the entrance to New York Harbour, holding a torch in her left hand and a flat stone with 4 July 1776 carved on it – the date of the *Declaration of Independence* – in her right hand. It was a present to the people of America from the people of France in 1886. The French started a collection to pay for it after the American Civil War (1861–5), which was fought, in part, over the issue of freeing black slaves.

Source B

This is part of the American *Declaration of Independence*:

All men are created equal, God has given them rights which cannot be taken away. Among these are the right to life, liberty and the pursuit of happiness. When any government threatens these rights the people can alter or abolish it and set up a new government.

The head of the Statue of Liberty, in an exhibition in Paris. The statue was originally called 'Liberty Enlightening the World'.

Why did they do it?

The statue was said to be a celebration of liberty. It was a reminder that the French had fought for liberty, inspired by the stand the Americans had made in 1776. It was also a congratulation to the winners of the Civil War, whom the French saw as fighting for liberty – the liberty of black slaves in the South. It was also a piece of advertising for France. It said, in 46 metres of beaten copper, 'we believe in Liberty'. The world may well have needed the reminder. Only a few years earlier, in 1871, the French government had put a stop to a revolution in Paris with great brutality.

Ideas and reality

The words at the foot of the Statue of Liberty say:
Give me your tired, your poor
Your huddled masses, yearning to breathe free,
The wretched refuse of your teeming shore.
Send these, the homeless, tempest-tossed to me.
I lift my lamp beside the golden door.

The words summed up America to many Europeans. It was a land of opportunity, a place where the poor, homeless and hopeless of an over-crowded Europe could make a fresh start, and prosper.

But by the end of the nineteenth century America was feeling overwhelmed by immigrants, especially the poor and homeless. By 1892 the steady stream was a flood. A new site was needed to 'process' immigrants. From this point on it got harder to enter the USA, although no official limits were placed on the number of people who could enter the country until the 1920s. They were inspected on the ship. Any with serious infectious diseases could not leave. The rest were shipped to Ellis Island, soon called 'the isle of tears' in several languages. At Ellis Island people were examined and inspected. Doctors chalked letters on their clothes to show if they had heart disease or rickets, or were feeble-minded. People with chalked letters on their clothes were shipped back to the boats. The rest carried on being processed by officials, who were rushed off their feet. Those who finally got landing cards often entered America with a different name – the closest the official could get to their real one.

Source C

In 1852, a free black man, Frederick Douglass, was asked to give the 4th of July speech in Independence Day celebrations. The people who asked him were startled by his reply, which pointed out that many states still actively supported slavery.

Pardon me, and allow me to ask, but why am I called here today? This Fourth of July is yours, not mine. To drag a man in chains to the temple of liberty and call on him to rejoice with you – are you mocking me? Over your joy I hear the mournful wail of millions, whose chains, heavy yesterday, are made more unbearable by celebrations all around the nation today.

The American Civil War (1861–5)

The American Civil War was a war between the northern and southern states of America. Slavery was one of the issues that sparked the war.

The southern states believed that they had every right to have black slaves. The economy of the south rested on the earnings of cotton plantations, which could not have been run without slave labour. The northern states had declared against slavery.

However, the main problem was how much the federal government could interfere in the way states ran their local affairs. The southern states saw slavery as a local issue. The northern states saw it as a national one.

3.4 THE FRENCH REVOLUTION

Why did the French Revolution break out in 1789?

All kinds of causes

There was not one cause for the French Revolution. There were many. Some causes had been brewing for some time. Other causes were more recent. These long and short term causes all added together to make a revolution more and more likely, until it got to a point where anything could have set it off.

Rich and poor

The gap between rich and poor had been growing wider for years. It was most obvious in the cities, especially Paris, where the rich and poor lived side by side. Things were worse in years when the harvests were bad. Then there was not enough corn, so the price of bread went up sharply. The 1780s had several bad harvests in a row. The harvest of 1788 was the worst yet, and the price of bread had doubled.

Running the country

France was divided into three groups – the First Estate (churchmen), the Second Estate (rich and important people) and the Third Estate (everyone else, from rich shopkeepers to homeless beggars). While the Third Estate did most work, they did not have a say in how France was run. But they were expected to pay taxes – more than the other two Estates.

ROBESPIERRE

Robespierre was part of the Revolution from its early days. At first, he seemed to support moderate reforms, as many people did at the time. It was not until late 1793 that he made it clear that he saw ruling by terror as a necessary way to govern. In the months that followed he became more and more suspicious of everyone, even his close advisers. It was the changes he made to the law, allowing people to be arrested if simply 'suspected' of a crime, that led his enemies to arrest and execute him in 1794.

The storming of the Bastille prison, 14 July 1789.

Source A

In 1789 the French king had to call the Estates General (a meeting of representatives of the three estates) because the government was in debt and he needed more taxes. Kings only did this when desperate for money – the last Estates General had been in 1614! When it met, the Third Estate demanded a say in how the country was run. The King refused. The cartoon shows what happened next.

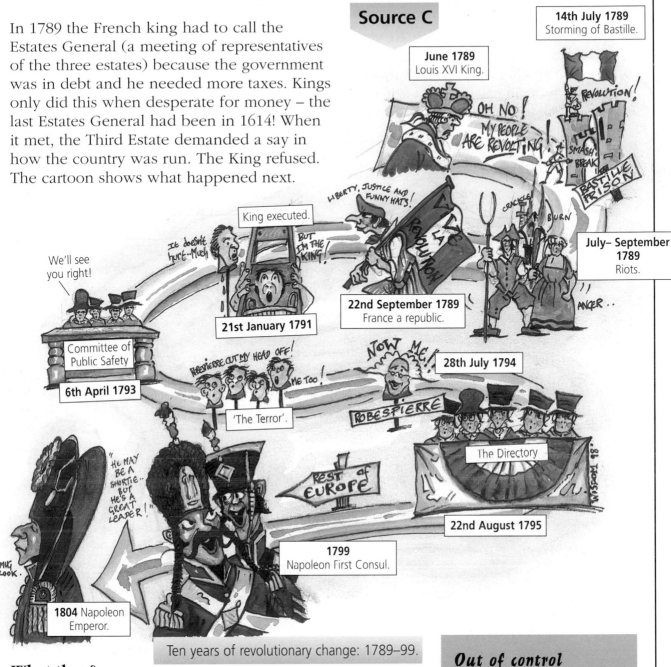

Ten years of revolutionary change: 1789–99.

What then?

After the fall of Robespierre, a more moderate government took control. In 1795 they set up the Directory, a five-man council that ran things with the help of Parliament. They undid most of the work of the Revolutionary Government, good and bad. They stopped any resistance by using the army. One army leader quickly became powerful. As the Directory relied on the army more and more, so his power grew. By 1799 he was powerful enough to throw out the Directory and take over France. His name was Napoleon Bonaparte. You can read about him on pages 84–7.

Out of control

On 22 June 1789 the Third Estate of the *parlement* formed the National Assembly. They did not want to get rid of the monarchy but simply to have a fair constitution. After the storming of the Bastille, the National Assembly tried to keep control. But there was rioting all over France, and food shortages. Things slid out of control.

What happened after the Revolution?

What was Paris like immediately after the Revolution? An Englishwoman called Helen Williams lived there and wrote a book about it. Here are some extracts.

Growing suspicion

From the moment the Revolutionary Government came to power the atmosphere in Paris thickened with growing suspicion. Every day fresh plots were discovered. They were laid at the door of nobles, priests, bankers and foreigners. Now that the phrase 'suspected' came into use – you could be arrested on suspicion of being involved in a plot, with no proof against you at all. The members of the Revolutionary Tribunal protested at the broad sweep of this. They were accused of 'moderation' and replaced with men who were willing to do as they were told. The Revolutionary Government also decided that revolutionary committees should be set up all over the country to make sure their decrees were carried out. There were fears that the revolutionary committees in the countryside might not be active enough, so a revolutionary army was set up to go around the country, checking up on the committees.

Imprisonment

Rumours abounded. We were told English residents would not be harmed. Then we were told we would be arrested and have our property taken. The days passed. More and more of our friends were arrested. Yet the local revolutionary committee did not arrest us. We began to think that, as a family of women, we would be spared. But this was a time when neither age nor sex won you compassion. We were woken in the middle of the night by a loud knocking on the door. Two soldiers and two representatives of the revolutionary committee had come to arrest us.

Helen Williams should not have been surprised that the Revolutionary Government acted against the English, who had been against the Revolution, even in its early days. This cartoon was printed in England in 1792.

Source D

Un petit Souper, a la Parisiènne:____or____A Family of Sans-Culotts refreshing, after the fatigues of the day.

WHO WAS HELEN WILLIAMS?

Helen Williams was an Englishwoman who went to live in Paris in 1788, when she was 26 years old. She was in favour of ideas of liberty and equality that she found flourishing there, and wrote letters home saying so. She was friendly with many people who had wanted to reform France. She had approved of the Revolution. She was horrified when events got out of control. Many of her friends were executed. She wrote letters to the English newspapers about what was happening. This made her fear that she, too, would go to the guillotine as an 'enemy of the people'. She eventually escaped to Switzerland, returning when the Terror was over.

While Helen Williams told the truth about Paris after the Revolution as she saw it, she did gloss over the reforms made by the Revolutionary Government, like providing free education and fixing the prices of basic foods. This is hardly surprising because she was strongly against the Revolutionary Government.

A kind of freedom

My sister's French fiancé got us released. But we were watched. We went out little. We were terrified we would break some new law and get arrested. There were spies everywhere. We jumped at each knock at the door, fearing arrest. Prisons grew daily more crowded. More and more people went to the scaffold as the Terror tightened its grip. One person was arrested because he 'looked noble', another because a total stranger said he supported the monarchy. Some were arrested for being too clever, others for being too rich. Others were given no reason at all.

The guillotine

As the numbers of executions rose, the horrors increased. Stories of courage and cowardice passed from home to home. You heard of one person taking another's place on the scaffold to save them. Others were less courageous. Madame du Barry, once the mistress of the King, had to be dragged every inch of the way to the scaffold. The screaming seemed to go on forever. Paris was a slaughterhouse. The guillotine claimed innocent and guilty alike, at such a rate that the gutters seemed to stream with blood.

Rising terror

Robespierre seemed mad with power. No one, not even his closest friends, felt safe. We were told to leave Paris in ten days, or go to trial. This meant the scaffold. So we left. We managed to get special passes to return to Paris. This saved our lives for, soon after we returned, a decree was passed ordering all nobles and foreigners outside Paris to be executed. Paris itself was far from safe. You could be arrested 'on suspicion of being suspected' now. Most people watched the processions of death with stupefied horror. What could they do? They could not stop the executions. Even to show horror or sympathy would put their foot on the steps to the scaffold, their neck beneath the blade of the guillotine. Life was so difficult and dangerous that many killed themselves.

Émigrés

Émigrés were French people who left France before or during the Revolution and went to live in another country. Many came to England. There were two main waves of émigrés – many nobles left immediately after the storming of the Bastille, rightly fearing for their lives. They were allowed, even encouraged, to leave.

In 1792 there was a second wave of émigrés; many were professional people who had supported the revolution at first, but were concerned at the course it was taking. They were not encouraged to leave; they had to take huge risks to escape. Those who were caught trying to escape were usually executed.

Who was Napoleon?

Napoleon Bonaparte is perhaps France's most famous historical figure, but he was very nearly Italian and not French! The island of his birth, Corsica, was an Italian possession until 1768 when it was taken over by the French. One year later Napoleon was born, the second son of a local lawyer. He was raised speaking Italian, but was sent to be educated in France. He won a scholarship to the élite military school in Paris and took just one year to pass the two-year course.

When the Revolution broke out in 1789 Napoleon was in Paris. Four years later, he commanded the gunners defending the southern city of Toulon against an English attack. The Revolutionary Government was so impressed that he received several promotions (of course, some army officers had fled during the Revolution, so there were vacancies!). In 1795 he defeated a pro-Royalist revolt in Paris and was rewarded by being promoted to Major General. He soon won a series of battles against the Austrians and in 1798 defeated the Egyptians at the Battle of the Pyramids. Back in Paris people heard stories of the brave deeds of their great general and Napoleon became a household name.

Napoleon takes control

Whilst in Egypt, Napoleon heard that the government in France was having difficulties. He returned to Paris and soon decided that France needed stronger government. He convinced the Directory that he was loyal to it and was made commander of the troops in Paris. But really he was plotting against it, and two days later, on 11 November 1799 he used the army to seize power. The Directory was overthrown and replaced by a government headed by three **consuls**. Napoleon was to be First Consul, which really meant that he ran the country. This was shown five years later when he had himself crowned Emperor in the cathedral of Notre Dame in Paris.

Source A

Comments made by Napoleon during the preparation of the Code Napoleon.

The husband must possess the absolute power and right to say to his wife 'Madam you shall not go to the theatre, you shall not entertain such and such a person.' Women should stick to knitting.

Napoleon might have been Emperor of France, but that did not mean that he was exempt from everyday illness. Here is a list of his medical problems.

- Constipation and piles
- Pain when urinating
- Scars and pain from old battle wounds
- A disease which caused shrinking of the penis
- Stomach cancer (which eventually killed him)

A painting of Napoleon crowning himself Emperor in 1804. Napoleon has taken the crown and is placing it on his own head. The artist, David, was Napoleon's Chief Painter.

Josephine (1763–1814)

Marie Josephine Rose Tascher de la Pagerie was the first wife of Napoleon Bonaparte. She was born in the French possession of Martinique in the West Indies, and her first husband was guillotined during the Great Terror in 1794. Two years later she married Napoleon. In 1804, when he became emperor, she was made empress of France. Her marriage to Napoleon ended when he divorced her in 1809 because of her alleged infertility, though she had given birth to a son and a daughter during her first marriage.

Napoleon in power

In 1789 Napoleon had claimed to support the Revolution, but though he is famous for his reforms there were many ways in which his rule was not in keeping with the ideas of 'liberty and equality'.

- Napoleon had himself crowned as Emperor. During the Revolution, the King had been beheaded.
- Napoleon also gave noble titles to his family and in 1808 created an Imperial nobility of senior French aristocrats. The Revolution had abolished the nobility.
- During the Revolution many churches were closed down and France 'de-Christianised'. Napoleon agreed to allow Catholics to worship openly once more, but he insisted that he, not the Pope, should appoint bishops.
- Although Napoleon allowed all men to vote, once he became Emperor there were no more elections.
- Napoleon did not allow freedom of speech. He censored newspapers and set up a secret police force to control his opponents. The Revolution had banned censorship, though it was used during the Terror (1793–5).

But Napoleon is known in France as a great reformer and some of his reforms were in keeping with the spirit of the Revolution.

- In 1804 he introduced the Code Napoleon. This was a clear statement of the laws of France. It said that all people were equal before the law and there were no special privileges for rich people. But it also said wives had to be obedient to husbands.
- Napoleon reformed the education system, placing more emphasis on science and mathematics and introducing a new type of school, the *lycée*, run on military lines.
- Napoleon wanted Paris to be a fitting capital for an emperor and spent money on new buildings in the city.

Napoleon the warrior

Napoleon is best remembered as a great military general who conquered almost all of Europe and made France the most powerful country in the world. When Napoleon came to power, France was at war with Austria, Britain and Russia. Napoleon defeated the Austrians at the Battle of Marengo in 1800 and forced them to sign a peace treaty agreeing that the French should control Holland, Switzerland and parts of Italy. Austria's allies, Britain and Russia, also made peace.

But by 1803 France was at war with Britain again. The British feared that Napoleon was becoming too powerful and that he intended to threaten the British Empire. Napoleon decided to invade Britain and put an end to its opposition to him. In 1804 an army was stationed along the French coast ready to invade. Napoleon had to be sure that his navy was strong enough to control the Channel and protect his soldiers as they crossed. But in October 1805 Admiral Nelson led the British navy to victory over a combined Spanish and French fleet at the Battle of Trafalgar. Napoleon decided to call off his invasion plans.

Source C

The rule of the Bonapartes in Europe.

France	– ruled by Napoleon
Spain	– ruled by Joseph (Napoleon's brother)
Holland	– ruled by Louis (Napoleon's brother)
Italy	– ruled by Eugene (Napoleon's stepson)
Westphalia	– ruled by Jerome (Napoleon's brother)
Gustalla	– ruled by Pauline (Napoleon's sister)
Lucca	– ruled by Elisa (Napoleon's sister)
Naples	– ruled by Joachim (Napoleon's brother-in-law)

Source D

The flight of Napoleon at Waterloo. His élite force of Old Guard are clearing the way for him.

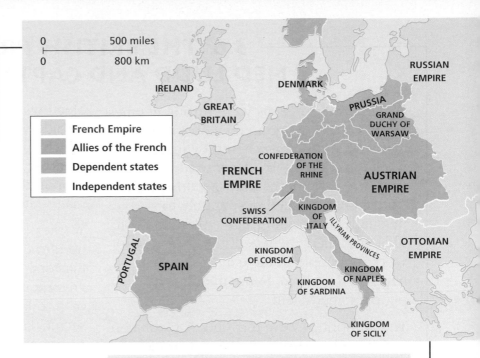

Europe in 1810.

Problems

In 1805 Russia, Prussia and Austria joined Britain against France, but they were soon defeated. By 1810 Napoleon controlled almost all of Europe. He set up the Continental System, forbidding countries under French control to trade with Britain. He wanted to force the British to make peace. But soon things started to go wrong.

In 1808 the King of Spain died. Napoleon decided to make his brother king instead of the rightful heir, Ferdinand. Soon France was at war with Spain and its neighbour, Portugal. Napoleon had expected this and thought that 12,000 men would be enough to win this Peninsular War. In the end he had an army of 300,000 soldiers and still lost. The British sent troops led by the Duke of Wellington to help the Spanish and by 1813 Napoleon's troops had been driven back into France.

More defeats

Napoleon invaded Russia in the summer of 1812, and reached Moscow in September. But as the Russians retreated, they burned everything of value – especially food. Soon Napoleon realised that he would have to pull out of Russia. As his men began their long retreat, winter fell and thousands died from the cold.

Napoleon had taken an army of over 600,000 men into Russia. Only 50,000 made it back to France.

Final defeat

By 1814 Napoleon's position was so weak that he was forced to surrender to his enemies. He was deposed and the old king's son was reinstated as Louis XVIII. Napoleon was sent to live in exile on the island of Elba off the coast of Italy. But he escaped in 1815 and returned to Paris. He was welcomed by huge crowds who wanted to see a return to the glorious days when France controlled Europe. But it was not to be. Napoleon was defeated by the combined forces of Austria, Russia, Prussia and Britain at Waterloo on 18 June 1815. He surrendered again and was sent into exile on St Helena, an island 8000 km from France. He died there in 1821.

Admiral Nelson (1758–1805)

Horatio Nelson was a British naval commander, famous for his victory over the French at Trafalgar. He led the attack in the *Victory*, but was wounded and died as the battle was nearing its end.

3.6 THE BRITISH PROTEST: NED LUDD AND CAPTAIN SWING

The 1750s to 1850s were turbulent times in Britain. Working men and women marched and rioted when they feared they would lose their jobs. They tried to combine into unions to protect themselves. Above all, they tried desperately to persuade Parliament to give them the vote. This was, many believed, the only way for working people to have a say in what happened to them. Some middle-class people joined them.

The authorities were terrified. A revolution in France had overturned a government and beheaded a king. Could the same happen in Britain? The government did all it could to clamp down.

Source A

Foster's Mill was a Yorkshire woollen mill which was set on fire by the Luddites in 1812. This is a song written about the mill at the time.

Come all you **croppers** stout and bold.
Let your faith grow stronger still;
Oh the cropper lads in the County of York,
They broke the shears at Foster's Mill.

The wind it blew, the sparks they flew,
Which alarmed the town full soon;
And out of bed poor people did creep
And run by the light of the moon.

Around and around they all did stand
And solemnly did swear.
Neither bucket nor kit, nor any such thing,
Should be of assistance there.

Around and around we all did stand
And sternly swear we will.
We'll break the shears and windows too,
And set fire to the **tazzling mill**.

Croppers:	men who trimmed the surface of cloth.
Tazzling mill:	a machine which raised the surface of the cloth before it was trimmed.

Meetings of more than 50 people were forbidden. A tax was put on pamphlets which spread revolutionary ideas, so working people couldn't afford them. Wide 'stop and search' powers were given to magistrates.

Workers in all sorts of trades and industries tried to combine together against their masters. In 1797 MPs made it a crime for anyone who joined a society to swear an oath to keep its rules and members' names secret. They then passed laws forbidding *any* combination of workmen. This didn't, of course, mean that workmen stopped combining into unions and societies. They simply had to do it in secret.

Ned Ludd

Hundreds of workers were afraid that new machinery would put them out of work. They took their revenge on the machines and broke them up. They also burned down the mills and factories which housed the machines. Sometimes they issued warnings, signed by 'Ned Ludd'.

Source B

From a letter sent to a Huddersfield master in 1812.

SIR

Information has just been given that you are a holder of these detestable Shearing Frames. You will take notice that if they are not pulled down by the end of next week, I shall detach one of my lieutenants with at least 300 men to destroy them. We will increase your misfortunes by burning your buildings down to ashes, and if you fire at any of my men, they have orders to murder you. Have the goodness to go to your neighbours and inform them that the same fate awaits them if their Frames are not taken down.

Signed by the General of the Army of Redressers

Ned Ludd

This picture ,'The Home of the Rick Burner', was published in the magazine *Punch* in 1844.

The machine-breakers came to be called 'Luddites'. The machine-breaking began in Nottingham in 1811 (where some masters had set up large knitting frames which could be worked by unskilled men) and quickly spread to Yorkshire, Cheshire and Lancashire. The government moved swiftly and passed a law which said that the death penalty could be passed on anyone found guilty of machine-breaking.

Captain Swing

Many farmers in the south and east of Britain introduced threshing machines. These could do the work of several men and took away winter employment. This caused great misery for labourers and their families, especially when allowances paid to help the poor were cut in the 1820s. In 1830, labourers' anger exploded. They burned **hayricks** and smashed threshing machines throughout the south of England. Threshing machines were destroyed in counties as far apart as Norfolk and Devon, Hereford and Sussex. As the unrest spread, ricks were burned to the ground in almost all English counties from Lancashire to Dorset, from Yorkshire to Surrey.

Source D

A 'Swing' letter, threatening to burn down a school. Presumably the owner was a supporter of the new machinery.

Sometimes farmers were sent threatening notes signed by 'Captain Swing'. Some farmers attempted to agree terms with the Swing rioters before their own crops or property were destroyed; all farmers condemned 'Captain Swing'.

The government and the judges took a firm line: 19 labourers were executed, 481 were transported to Australia and 644 were sent to prison.

Crime and punishment

At the beginning of the 19th century there were over 200 crimes which could be punished by death. These included:

- treason
- rebellion
- murder
- stealing goods worth more than £2
- cutting down trees without permission
- sending threatening letters
- sheep stealing
- damaging Westminster Bridge
- pretending to be a Chelsea pensioner.

Executions were carried out in public. The last public execution was in 1868.

Between 1839 and 1842, gangs of angry people attacked toll gates on turnpike roads (see page 62) in west Wales. They pulled the gates down, burned them and sometimes destroyed the toll-keeper's house, too. Wages were low and many farm labourers were struggling even to feed their families. Farmers themselves were in difficulties because oats and barley, sheep and pigs were fetching very low prices at market. Having to pay turnpike tolls was, for many, a final blow.

Twm Carnabwth and Efailwen

On the night of 6 June 1839 a local farmer called Twm Carnabwth (Thomas Rees) led a heavily disguised gang to the toll gates at Efailwen in north Pembrokeshire. They carried burning torches, crowbars, sledge-hammers, scythes and axes. When they had finished there was nothing left of the toll-gates or the toll-keeper's house but rubble and burnt-out timbers. What made this protest different? Twm and those with him were wearing women's clothes and some of them had blackened their faces, too!

Some people say Twm borrowed his clothes from a woman called Rebecca; others that the rioters said their leader was called Rebecca because of a verse in the Bible (see Source A). Whatever the reason, all future attacks on toll-gates were led by 'Rebecca'. No one knows whether there was just one leader or whether anyone leading a toll-gate riot was really called 'Rebecca'.

TWM CARNABWTH (1806–76)

An agricultural labourer, Twm lived at Carnabwth, Mynachlogddu with his wife Rachel and children Elizabeth, Daniel and John. He was a religious man and regularly recited biblical texts at chapel festivals. But he was also a prizefighter. His body was covered in scars and he lost an eye in one fight. It was sometimes difficult to keep him sober! He was always ready to take part in the *Ceffyl Pren*, which was a Welsh custom of frightening people who had offended against the moral code of the community.

Source A

This extract from the Bible comes from Genesis XXIV verse 60.

And they blessed Rebecca, and said unto her, Thou art our sister. Be thou the mother of thousands of millions, and let thy seed possess the gates of those that hate them.

Source B

A picture called *Rebecca and Her Daughters* painted in the nineteenth century.

Was there just one 'Rebecca'?

Many people believed that whoever was leading an attack on Welsh toll-gates dressed as a woman and called themselves 'Rebecca'. Some people, however, believe that there was just one 'Rebecca' and that this was Hugh Williams, who:

- was a respected lawyer and landowner
- said he was one of the first people to take notice of the toll-gate problem in 1838
- defended many Rebecca rioters who came before magistrates
- attended a mass meeting of miners, coal dealers and farmers on Mynydd Sylen in 1843 where he agreed to draw up a petition to Queen Victoria setting out all the causes of the rioting
- told a friend that he was the 'instigator and undiscovered leader of the Rebecca movement'.

A drawing of the Rebecca rioters made at the time.

Dai'r Cantwr and Shoni Sgubor Fawr

The Rebecca riots quietened down until 1842, when they flared up again all over west Wales. Two leaders were Dai'r Cantwr and Shoni Sgubor Fawr. Shoni was a tough, hard-drinking ex-soldier and prizefighter. Dai'r was an ex-miner, ballad singer and Methodist preacher. Together with their followers, they destroyed toll-gates and threatened and robbed wherever they went. The authorities were forced to ask for help and soldiers restored law and order. Ordinary rioters were rarely caught, but Dai'r and Shoni were betrayed, captured and sent for trial. They pleaded guilty and were sentenced to transportation. They laughed as they were sentenced.

Source C

Part of a letter sent to a newspaper *The Welshman* on 1 September 1843.

The people are with me. They are all my children. When I meet the lime men on the road covered with sweat and dust, I know they are Rebeccaites. When I see the coalmen coming to town clothed in rags, hard worked and hard fed, I know they are mine, they are Rebecca's children. When I see the farmers' wives carrying loaded baskets to market, bending under the weight, I know well they are my daughters. If I turn into a farmer's house and see them eating barley bread and drinking whey, surely, say I, these are members of my family, these are the oppressed sons and daughters of Rebecca.

Source D

The end of turnpikes

By 1830, 3500 km of roads had been turnpiked and there was a good road network connecting the main towns and cities in Great Britain. But soon a threat to the turnpikes was to become a reality. No one could stop the spread of the railways. Gradually the Turnpike Trusts lost money as more people travelled and sent their goods by train. By the 1880s, nearly all the Trusts had been disbanded. In the 1880s and 1890s, various laws gave responsibility for road repairs to county councils and local councils.

3.8 THE BRITISH PROTEST: THE CHARTISTS

In the years after 1832, leaflets demanding the six points of the People's Charter (Source A) appeared on the streets of Birmingham, Glasgow, Leeds, Liverpool and London. Why was this?

Many working people had hoped that the Reform Act of 1832 would give them the vote. The vote, they believed, was the only way to get a fairer deal for themselves. That way they could elect working people as MPs and their voice would be heard properly in Parliament. But they were badly disappointed. Parliament was still dominated by the wealthy. Many working people wanted change, and they wanted it quickly. So they gave their support to the People's Charter and became Chartists.

Who joined the Chartists?

People who became Chartists were craftsmen like printers and cabinet makers, factory workers like cotton spinners and home-workers like woolcombers, handloom weavers and framework knitters. Some who joined turned to Chartism only when times were bad. Others remained Chartists all their lives.

Source A

The People's Charter:

1 **A vote for every man over 21 years of age**

2 **A secret ballot**

3 **No property qualification for MPs**

4 **Payment for MPs**

5 **Equal-sized constituencies**

6 **Annually elected parliaments.**

The Chartists sent three huge petitions to Parliament asking for the Charter to be granted. They said that the first petition (in 1839) contained one million signatures, the second (in 1842) contained three million signatures and the third (in 1848) contained six million signatures. Parliamentary officers looked carefully at the signatures on the last petition. They found signatures like 'Queen Victoria', 'Pug-face' and 'Flat-nose'. In this picture, the procession is taking the 1842 petition to Parliament.

Source B

Physical force Chartists

Holding rallies and collecting signatures on petitions are reasonably peaceful ways of making a point to those in authority. Not all Chartists thought this was the answer.

In 1839, after the first petition had been rejected by Parliament, Chartists in Halifax and Wakefield, Bradford and Leeds armed themselves with sticks, **cudgels** and sometimes guns and began practising drill in secret on the moors. Frightened of an armed rebellion, the government put General Napier in charge of 500 soldiers and gave him responsibility for keeping law and order in the north. In the same year John Frost led an armed gang of miners and iron-workers to release a fellow Chartist from gaol in Newport. Twenty-four people were killed in the battle which followed.

Source C

The Chartists had several leaders at different times and in different places. However, the two most important national leaders were William Lovett and Feargus O'Connor.

We have resolved to obtain our rights, peacefully if we may, forcibly if we must.
(Feargus O'Connor)

Muskets are not what is wanted, but education and schooling of the working people.
Before an educated people a government must bow.
(William Lovett)

Source D

This rather fuzzy photograph is the world's earliest known news photograph. It shows the Chartist rally on Kennington Common, London, in 1848. Chartists used rallies to help gain public support and to keep people aware of what they wanted.

Getting the six points?

- In 1872 all voting in general elections was made secret.

- In 1885, there was a major re-distribution of parliamentary seats: 159 old seats were taken away and 175 new ones created, helping make constituencies of equal size.

- In 1911 salaries were paid to MPs for the first time. They were given £400 a year.

- In 1911, the longest a parliament could 'sit' was reduced from seven to five years. There was no suggestion that parliaments should 'sit' for one year only.

- In 1918, all men over the age of 21 were given the vote.

- In 1928, all women over the age of 21 were given the vote.

abolitionists people who wanted slavery abolished, and who campaigned for this cause.

acquitted not found guilty.

apprentice someone who is learning a trade by working for a master for a certain period of time or for very low wages, sometimes no wages at all, just food and lodgings.

aristocrats members of the highest class in society.

blight a plant disease caused by fungus or insects.

brimstone an early word for sulphur, a yellow chemical element.

carding the action of 'combing' wool which has come straight from the fleece, to make it free from tangles so it can be spun.

chaff the husks around the grains of crops, that are separated by shaking.

Chartist someone who believed in the Chartism movement for social and electoral reform in the mid-nineteenth century.

commissions groups set up by the government to investigate issues.

confirmation a religious ritual, confirming a baptised person as a member of the Christian Church.

consul a chief magistrate, appointed to head the government.

cudgels short, thick sticks, used as weapons.

depots storehouses.

domestic service working as a servant in a household, for example, scullery maid or cook.

drayman someone who drives a horse and cart for a brewer.

emigrated left your country of birth to live in another country.

entrepreneur someone who gets involved in lots of businesses and enterprises, with the risk of profit or loss.

epidemic a disease that kills a lot of people in one outbreak.

evicted made to leave one's rented home, because of non-payment of rent.

excursion trains trains that were intended to take people on journeys for pleasure, not business.

floggings beatings with a whip or stick as punishment.

gauze a fine mesh of wire that lets light through.

goods produce of a country, which can be traded.

guillotine a machine with a heavy, sharp blade that drops down, used for beheading.

hayricks another word for a haystack – a packed pile of hay with a pointed top.

hearse the vehicle that carries the coffin at a funeral.

hovels small, roughly-made houses, usually with only one room, made from mud and straw, and thatched.

indenture a settled agreement or contract between an apprentice and employer.

independence freedom for a country to rule itself, and not be under the authority of another country.

indigo a natural blue dye, which comes from the indigo plant.

inoculation giving someone a very small dose of a disease, so they can build up immunities to that disease, preventing them from getting it again.

ironworks a factory where iron goods are made.

keep food and lodgings.

knighted awarded a title by a monarch, in return for good service.

liberty freedom.

marines a body of troops trained to serve on land or sea.

martyrs people who are punished because of their beliefs.

mechanisation the introduction of machines to do factory work, instead of manual labour.

morality a set of moral 'rules' which people consider to be right and proper.

music hall an evening of music and entertainment at a theatre or hall.

penal colony a colony to which people are **transported** as a punishment from the country which owns the colony.

pitching rolling and lurching violently from one side to another.

plantations estates, usually in colonies, on which tobacco, cotton, sugar and other products are grown. Plantations were usually worked on by slaves.

planters the managers of **plantations.**

plundering robbing a place of its goods, especially in war.

reformers people who wanted reform. People who wanted things to change according to their ideals.

repealed withdrawn from law.

revolution the overthrow of a government in favour of a new system.

scullery a small room, usually at the back of the kitchen, used for washing dishes and pots.

seed potatoes those potatoes which are grown for planting again next year, not for eating.

socialist someone who believes that the community as a whole should control production and distribution of goods.

sub-let allow somebody to rent property from you, when you are renting the property in the first place.

telephone exchange the central telephone office, where calls are taken and transferred.

transported sent to a **penal colony** instead of prison, as a punishment.

Viceroy someone who rules on behalf of a monarch if the monarch does not live in that country.

workhouses houses where people who were too poor to support themselves were sent, to work for their **keep**. Workhouses were made as uncomfortable as possible, in an attempt to make them unattractive to idle people.

INDEX